What to do in a school crisis

Crisis Relief

From chaos to calm
A teacher's guide

Step 1 : open book

By certified psychologists

Peter F. White, MA;
David W. Peat, PhD

Trafford
PUBLISHING® www.trafford.com
North America & international
toll-free: 1 888 232 4444 (USA & Canada)
fax: 812 355 4082

Preface

Developing a workable, meaningful school and/or community crisis plan is not simply a task for large urban schools. There is a need for all schools and communities to have such a plan in place. Increasingly schools must cope with student fights, weapons in the school, drug abuse, gangs, and other forms of violent behaviors that are not exclusive to the larger city schools. Schools mirror the wider society; therefore, much of the information contained in this manual also applies to communities.

Although it is not possible to completely protect children or a school from these issues, a comprehensive and collaboratively developed crisis plan can go a long way to relieving the adverse effects that traumatic events can have on the lives of children. It has been consistently proven that prior crisis planning can make a significant difference when an emergency happens. In short, planning and learning about crisis relief, in advance allows teachers to create calm even during the chaos of a crisis. When a comprehensive strategy is in place, school staff can more effectively and responsibly protect children and lessen the impact of a traumatic event. Recent history has shown us that planning for large-scale disasters due to natural causes such as hurricanes, cyclones, floods, tsunamis or man-made catastrophic events, needs to be undertaken.

This manual was developed by both authors from involvement in specific workshops and clinics on crisis intervention and suicide prevention, coupled with extensive first-hand experience responding to numerous crises and traumatic events in both urban and rural schools located in the Yukon Territory of Canada, Singapore, Maldives and Haiti. Thank you from both Peter White and Dr. David Peat to the people of Maldives for their contribution to the development of portions of this manual during a training-of-trainers workshop following the tragic 2004 Indian Ocean tsunami and earthquake. We salute the resilience and kindness of the people of the Maldives, particularly the staff and directors of The Care Society, Male. As well, ActionAid's funding for the workshop and the on-going post-tsunami support for Maldivians and other vulnerable peoples of the world is greatly esteemed[1].

The authors would like to express sincere thanks and appreciation to all the teachers, principals, school staff, and community agencies that provided numerous suggestions after having supported them in one crisis or another.

---

1   A training manual was also produced from the original *Comprehensive Critical Incident Intervention* manual for the Care Society, Republic of Maldives. This training manual was collaboratively developed and contextualized by community care workers and other professionals working with victims of the Tsunami, including displaced families and individuals.

Thank you to Leona Zinn for her strong support and encouragement, without which this book would not have been completed. We would like to thank a true expert in the field of critical incident intervention and Peter's friend, Althea Woods, for her invaluable input and guidance drafting this manual. As well, we would like to thank Dr. Robert McClelland and Patricia McClelland for their excellent initial editing and advice and Stephen White for his vital proofreading. For this second edition, Barbara Kermode-Scott's editing, advice and support has been indispensable and much appreciated.

Peter F. White and David W. Peat

Table of Contents

WHAT TO DO

Step 1: Open the book and find the information you need

INTRODUCTION

Rather than pray your school will never be faced with a tragedy, major emergency, or crisis, plan for any event. If you should find you're in a crisis, you'll need to know what to do. Use this book as your guide.

It's always best to have a plan for traumatic events. You can prepare for all those nightmarish life and death situations you hope you'll never have to face.

Start by being proactive. Develop a school crisis intervention plan. We can help!

Too often, people respond to a crisis only once a critical incident is happening. Don't find yourself doing the same. Prepare now. Work with your colleagues and with local health, social services, and law enforcement agencies. Create intervention plans for a wide range of traumatic contingencies. Rehearse what you will do if a crisis should happen. Develop a crisis response plan for your community as well as your school. Discover how you can minimize the impact of a crisis on your students' behavioral, social, emotional, and academic lives.

In a crisis, you will need the help of experienced, highly trained personnel. Learn how to involve divisional/district personnel (school psychologists, counselors, and nurses) in your school. They will help you keep calm in any situation.

We have developed a ten-step plan to guide you. We suggest that you review the entire manual by flipping through the steps described below, so that you will know which ones to immediately go to if there is a classroom, school or community crisis.

We have also included various forms and checklists to help you record and track what you do and what needs to be done during a critical incident. You can use these forms and checklists to work with your colleagues and external advisors to start building a crisis plan for your school.

HOW THE BOOK IS ORGANIZED

The book is organized into chapters and appendixes, as follows:

- **Step 1: Open the book and find the information you need** - Provides the rationale for the manual and an overview of the procedures and strategies in the book.

- **Step 2: Prepare – Imagine the unimaginable** - Defines a crisis, presents an outline for selecting crisis team members and discusses how to develop a school-based crisis plan.

- **Step 3: Mobilize the school crisis team – now!** - Deals with the immediate response by a school crisis team. This step suggests the actions that should be taken, and recommends intervention strategies for kindergarten, elementary, and junior/senior students.

- **Step 4: Deal with the media and address parents' concerns** - Presents information about how school officials should respond to media attention and parental concerns. This step includes strategies that parents can implement to help their children cope with a traumatic event.

- **Step 5: Reduce traumatic stress – offer crisis counseling** - Consists of basic information necessary for conducting specific types of crisis counseling and ways of minimizing the short- and long-term negative effects of experiencing a traumatic event.

- **Step 6: Review the situation and "debrief"** - Presents a specific model for conducting classroom debriefings.

- **Step 7: Organize a memorial service – involve students** - Provides ideas concerning preparing students for a memorial service following a student or teacher's death (or multiple deaths), and presents suggestions for student involvement.

- **Step 8: Deal with crisis aftermath** - Discusses vicarious trauma, and provides guidelines for debriefing school staff, crisis response team members, and department personnel.

- **Step 9: Respond appropriately to different types of crises** - Reveals how to respond to specific traumatic events.

- **Step 10: Develop (or amend) a school crisis plan for the future** - Suggests how to develop a crisis plan that will meet the needs of your school.

- **Appendix 1: Pocket-sized reference cards** for each type of debriefing that is used as an intervention.

- **Appendix 2: Rapid response checklists** that can be used when responding to various crises and critical incidents or when you need to know what to do first.

ADAPTING THE INFORMATION FOR YOUR SCHOOL OR COMMUNITY SETTING

All forms and checklists in the appendixes of this manual may be copied. This should be of help to school administrators and community leaders as they develop a school or community-based critical incident intervention plan. Choose the checklists and forms tailored to your context (e.g., school, school-system or community) and develop a workable crisis plan or use for instructional or planning purposes.

Once a crisis plan has been developed and team members have been selected or appointed, all members should become familiar with the plan to ensure its smooth operation in the event of a crisis occurring. A school or community crisis intervention plan should be considered like a fire drill. For the plan to work effectively, everyone on the team must know the plan well. Periodically the plan should be reviewed and practiced, with changes made where necessary. Revisions and/or reviews should be recorded on the school/community incident plan review form. This will demonstrate a level of quality assurance for the school or community critical incident intervention plan. The original purchaser of this manual is permitted to copy, edit and contextualize all forms.

USING THE POCKET REFERENCE CARDS

Specific information from the manual has been prepared into small format lists (index card sized) in Appendix 1. These lists include: Defusing emotions, Group debriefing, Classroom debriefing, Individual debriefing, Operational debriefing and Suicide risk assessment. These lists are designed so that they can be carried in a pocket and accessed quickly and discreetly, to be used for a handy reference, as needed.

USING THE RAPID RESPONSE CHECKLISTS

Rapid response checklists are in Appendix 2. They are intended as a quick reference for use when a crisis occurs and you need to know the first steps. You can quickly determine whether an action has taken place by looking to see if it has been checked off or not. This provides a written record as to the action taken and the individual responsible for taking the action.

The first checklist (titled **Immediate response checklist**) outlines those steps that should be followed when responding to most critical incidents. Once the user has sufficient time, he or she should read the section(s) of the book that are pertinent to the situation at hand.

Step 2: Prepare – Imagine the unimaginable

TRAUMATIC EVENTS CAN AND DO TAKE PLACE AT SCHOOLS

Occasionally, teachers and students go to school to teach and learn but are faced with a life and death situation instead. The fear of a tragedy, a mass murder or massacre, is real. A suicide, whether on the premises or not, will also impact a school, as will a road traffic accident or other accident resulting in the death or injury of a teacher or student, or a major natural disaster.

The news media are constantly reporting violence in our schools. We've all heard about mass shootings, random attacks, stabbings, or incidents where a firearm has been discharged in a school, or on a school bus. Sometimes we recoil in horror when we hear a school has been the scene of multiple deaths. One of the worst incidents in recent memory was a mass shooting on the campus of Virginia Polytechnic Institute and State University in Blacksburg, Virginia. In April 2007, 32 students and faculty members at Virginia Tech were murdered. Another 17 students and faculty members were wounded. Violent attacks on schools are not simply a 21st century phenomenon. In 1927, Bath Consolidated School in Bath, Michigan, was bombed. The Bath School disaster remains the worst violent attack on a US school. The bombing resulted in the deaths of 38 elementary schoolchildren and six adults, as well as mass injuries.

Natural disasters also impact schools. The Louisiana Flood of 2016 affected many schools and displaced thousands of students. The 2011 Virginia Earthquake caused significant damage to public school buildings in Louisa County.

Fires occur on school premises daily.

You cannot always prevent a traumatic event impacting your school but you can prepare yourself, your staff, and your students for critical incidents.

Remember that trauma shatters the foundations of trust and order expected from authority. Students assume school is a safe environment comprised of people who care about them. When so many distraught individuals are obviously being ignored, their trust in the world is even further undermined. Their erratic behavior and emotional displays are difficult to contain. Control and routines are lost at a time when students need strong control coupled with deep understanding and compassion.

School staff should understand that the days following a sudden death or other traumatic event will be a time in which there is considerable confusion, with emotions running high. The levels of confusion and emotional reaction are a direct result of the traumatic event and the response by school personnel. It must be kept in mind that these factors will have a direct effect on the type and degree of intervention taken at the school.

A formal response to most crises lasts approximately three days, with a follow-up scheduled within two weeks and another one at six weeks. Crises affect everyone: teachers, administration, students, secretaries, and custodial staff. The purpose of any crisis intervention is to provide students and staff with a supportive atmosphere where they can express their feelings and fears openly and safely. The long-term goal of crisis intervention is to help students and staff members return to their pre-crisis level of functioning. This is achieved by helping individuals understand their reactions to the event and determine what they need to do next. Crisis intervention does not use psychotherapy or any other form of therapy. It does, however, attempt to strengthen defenses so individuals can deal with the existing and often overwhelming stress of the current situation. In addition, implementing crisis intervention procedures helps to reduce the potential effects of traumatic stress over a longer period.

Trauma in the literature

Trauma, at its core, is "an emotional wound with the possibility of the effects being long lasting" (Trethowan, 2009, p. 10). These long-lasting effects can manifest in psychological and/or physiological functioning (Flannery, 1999). For an event to cause trauma it must induce intense psychological discomfort that disrupts the individual's coping mechanisms (Briere, 2012); this leads to the emotional wound. Trauma-induced distress manifests variably across victims (APA, 2013). The most common symptoms of trauma are numbness, or a lack of feeling emotions and/or a state of general unease or dissatisfaction, outwardly expressed by anger/aggression, and behaviors that indicate a distorted perception of sights and sounds [paraphrased from APA (2013)]. The cause of trauma is complex and determined by a variety of risk-factors. Brock states that "psychological traumatization is the result of the interaction among the characteristics of the crisis event, individual crisis experiences, and personal resiliency, and vulnerability" (2002, p. 367). Risk factors for traumatization include social neglect (APA, 2013), negative perceptions, resiliency levels, connection to crisis victims, and crisis exposure itself (Brock, 2002). In children and adolescents, trauma has an impeding effect on the brain which negatively influences development, such as leaving the child with overreacting stress response systems (Stien and Kendall, 2004). Therefore, preventing trauma and reducing the negative effects of trauma are the areas of focus crisis interventions.

Reducing traumatic stress

Traumatic stress is an emotional crisis brought on by externally imposed stresses or situations that are unexpected, uncontrollable, and overwhelming. Individuals experiencing traumatic stress go through three stages: impulsive behavior, excessive depression, and possible psychotic breaks with anger often directed toward the school for not adequately addressing the situation.

The timeliness of providing support to individuals is critical. If people are not helped to discover a balanced resolution, they are left vulnerable to disorganization. If sufficient students and staff are affected, the entire school community itself is in danger of disorganization. These effects demonstrate why an effective crisis intervention plan is so important. It is not possible to predict all crises and when they will occur. A flexible and previously developed crisis plan will provide the appropriate response for students and staff during a critical incident.

Roberts mentions how one junior high school experienced the death of a student who was on the periphery of the student body (1990). The student was relatively unknown, and the school chose not to do anything to acknowledge his death. The teachers were forbidden to hold discussions with the students or comment about the incident.

Junior high schools probably have the most effective/efficient grapevine in the world, and within hours of the incident, all the students knew. They tried to whisper among themselves and contain their reactions in the classes but this proved to be beyond their ability because of their stage of development.

For days afterward, many students were in fights. Others cried with friends and were disciplined for not being where they should have been. Some started skipping school. Three days later, the school psychologists were called to work with the students. By this time, however, the anger of the grief process had been targeted toward the school, its teachers, and principal. Many teachers were ambivalent about ignoring the death and, through their anxiety, inadvertently communicated their own discomfort to the students. Although the psychologists did work in this school for quite some time, the school never regained the allegiance and the trust of these students.

SELECTING CRISIS TEAM MEMBERS

Recent literature and recommendations

Effective school crisis teams are essential to the management of crisis situations and emergencies at the school level. School crisis teams at their most basic function are meant to guide a school's response to crisis situations and emergencies both during and after (Knox and Roberts, 2005). These teams address areas of concern such as the mental health of students and staff, safety and medical priorities, facilities management, and communication (Villarreal and Peterson, 2015). A crisis team should be made up of members holding specific responsibilities and functions that they are familiar with and trained in (Nickerson et al., 2006). As well, it can be beneficial to have a school crisis team made up of team members who come from varying specializations and disciplines. Trethowan (2009) has found three overarching categories of skills that are perceived to be valuable for crisis intervention work.

The categories are:

- intervention skills
- theoretical knowledge
- administrative skills

Having a strong understanding of crisis and trauma theory will better inform a crisis team's intervention delivery while administrative coordination will help the team's efforts be consistent and effective. Additionally, every crisis team should have extra trained crisis personnel that can be called in to take the place of compromised team members (Knox and Roberts, 2005; Villarreal and Peterson, 2015). "A critical component of the success and maintenance of crisis teams is regular crisis team meetings outside of a crisis event" (Villarreal and Peterson 2015, p. 5). Therefore, crisis teams need to be tight-knit and focused. These factors should be kept in mind when choosing staff for them.

The best crisis teams are composed of people possessing a broad perspective on life. They should have an ability to perceive multiple consequences and a willingness to challenge an idea and then work cooperatively toward a solution. The ability to think clearly under stress, flexibility, and a familiarity with the subtleties of the school, its student body, and its community, are the most important attributes. Another characteristic that is desirable is a personal comfort level for discussing issues such as death and suicide. The crisis team often includes the principal, the vice-principal, the school counselor, a staff member, and a secretary. Other members may be added depending upon the size of the school and the nature of the crisis.

Assessing team preparedness

All team members must be trained in crisis intervention. The team members must know the plan thoroughly in their own school and should also be familiar with the plans at other schools where they may be expected to help. Team members must also be familiar with the strategies used for preventing post-traumatic stress disorder. It is most important that all team members continuously update their skills. The following questions will help to focus on the level of preparedness of your school based crisis response team.

- Who lacks training in individual and classroom debriefing, situational assessment, knowledge of post-traumatic stress disorder, and panic attacks?
- Where can this training be obtained?
- Has a school crisis plan been developed?
- If a school crisis plan has been developed, are all team members familiar with the plan and their responsibilities?
- Will the crisis team be expected to respond to all situations, including violence, death, natural disasters, and other accidents?
- Is any special equipment needed?

LEVELS OF RESPONSE TO A CRISIS

When a critical incident happens there will be at least two levels of response, school and district/division.

- The **school response** to a crisis tends to focus on direct intervention with students and staff.

- The **district/division response** to a school crisis tends to focus on indirect intervention and support to the affected school.

There are four situations when the district/division crisis team or individual members may be sent directly to a school.

- There is insufficient staff to make up a school-based crisis team at the affected school.

- It is district/division policy to dispatch crisis teams or individual members to the affected school.

- The school-based crisis team itself is in a crisis state (this state may arise if the death is the principal or a popular teacher).

- The principal has specifically requested the district/division crisis team or members to provide support to the school crisis team. The request may be made directly when it is imperative that crisis members come to the school immediately, or the principal may complete the **Critical incident intervention request**, located in Appendix 2 and submit it to the appropriate official. In many areas district/division crisis teams are not dispatched to schools unless specifically requested by the principal of the affected school. The community sees the principal as overseeing the school and ultimately responsible for the actions taken and avoided. This empowers the school crisis team and instills confidence in their ability. Specific checklists have been included (Appendix 2) to help track actions taken by school based crisis team personnel when a critical incident occurs. According to information from a small urban school district in Canada, responses at the school and department may include the following:

School-based response to crises

- will actively implement the school based crisis response plan

- will actively request assistance from the district/division crisis response team, if needed. This determination should be made by the principal in consultation with other members of the school crisis response team.

- will conduct such activities as defusing emotions, classroom debriefings, and crisis counseling

- will prepare an information letter to parents

- will conduct crisis response team and staff debriefings

- will provide a statement to the media providing information about actions taken at the school

- will monitor and coordinate all crisis response activities at the school

District/division response to crises

- will actively provide additional assistance to the school crisis response team, if requested by the principal of the affected school

- will actively request assistance from outside departments and sources, if necessary

- will contact all feeder schools with information about the incident

- will provide information to the media about actions taken by the district/division crisis response team following the incident

- will maintain close contact with the affected school

- will meet self-care needs of school staff, i.e. buying food, bringing in counselors, etc.

- will provide debriefing opportunities for all staff

- will conduct district/division level debriefing to evaluate the response to the crisis

"External" emergency support

This is a level of intervention whereby external crisis response members, e.g. district/division crisis response members, take a secondary role to the school crisis teams members when intervening in a critical incident. The school crisis team members are responsible for the implementation of individual and classroom debriefings. district/division crisis team members provide psychological support to the school team members and are available should school members get into difficulty dealing with individual questions and/or situations. External responders should take a secondary role to any school crisis team member, unless directed otherwise by the principal.

RECOGNIZING COMMUNITY EXPECTATIONS AROUND THE ROLE OF SCHOOLS

Petersen and Straub state that schools are incredibly influential in the daily lives of families within the community (1992). Often a great deal of the discipline and nurturing needed to raise sons or daughters centers on their life at school. Even parents who do not take an active interest in the school on a daily or regular basis have a silent interest in the school's environment as it affects their sons and daughters. Thus, the school becomes an effective and integral force within the community and in every family. For some children, it is the only source of safety and stability.

Today, schools are expected to address more than the academic and intellectual needs of students. Increasing emphasis is being placed upon the emotional, social, and physical needs of the students. Parents are beginning to look more to schools for the back-up support previously offered by the extended family.

The role of schools during and after a crisis

It is important to understand that it takes time to resolve a traumatic event. Calling in departmental and community specialists to help deal with the crisis is a good practice. Work with affected students must continue after the external consultants have returned to their offices. It is then up to the school to provide a constant and consistent support system for students. After a few days, most students will not need help, but some will require ongoing counseling and support to prevent post-traumatic stress disorder. It is important to note that the ongoing counseling differs from what is usually offered at the guidance office and what is available during the crisis. Quick intervention is a far more effective means to recovery than spending hours in a psychologist's office after the fact.

The importance of students' identification with the school is reflected in less delinquency, a lower dropout rate, and higher academic achievement. When crises and other traumatic events are not adequately resolved, they interfere with a student's acceptance of the school identity.

Likewise, precedents have already been set in court where school boards have been held liable for not adequately protecting the student and have been ordered to pay compensation. To protect the school, every crisis must be evaluated for possible liability. Through implementation of a school crisis intervention plan, the administration at the school will demonstrate that it is prepared to protect children during crises and other traumatic events.

Legal considerations for schools during and after a crisis

Liability

Schools are not subject to specific laws that require them to provide specialized services in the aftermath of a crisis. Implementing classroom debriefings attends to issues of legal, moral, and ethical importance. These issues directly concern the role of the school and behavior of school personnel. It is wise that school crisis response team members follow departmental/ divisional policy and procedures, direction from the school division's legal advisor, and their own professional judgment when attempting to meet students' needs during a crisis. Crisis teams and/or individual team members who engage in "freelancing" during a crisis may cause harm to the overall mission of the crisis team. To protect the school, every crisis must be evaluated for possible liability. If there is any doubt, check with the departmental/divisional solicitor. Crisis team members are well advised to remember that today we live in a litigious society. Often lawsuits are considered remedy. A lawsuit can be filed against anyone at almost any time and for just about any reason if a plaintiff feels that a personal wrong or injury has been caused. These lawsuits are brought under civil law.

Intervention, abandonment, and negligence

Unless a crisis team member has a preexisting duty to aid or intervene in another person's crisis, the law usually does not require that anyone intervene in the crisis of anyone else. Once an individual has started an intervention, that person must continue with the intervention unless relieved by someone with greater skill and ability. If the crisis team member does not continue with the intervention it may constitute abandonment, which could bring legal consequences. Negligence may occur when a crisis team member intervenes in the crisis of an individual but breaches that intervention, thus causing damage or further injury to the victim. "Good Samaritan" laws may protect individuals who intervene on behalf of those in a state of crisis. The intervention, however, must be reasonable and prudent. If it is not, negligence may occur.

Confidentiality

Another area of concern to school and district/divisional crisis response team members is the issue of confidentiality. It is important to note that various statutes regulate the collection, use, and disclosure of information by school boards and departments. The facts of each case will determine when it is legally appropriate to collect, use, and disclose personal information and to whom that information may be disclosed.

Disclosure of information and protection of privacy

It is important that you are aware of the legal frameworks in your jurisdiction that regulate the disclosure of information and the protection of privacy. There may be legislation in your area that restricts the collection and disclosure of written personal information by Boards and regulates the storage of such information.

Legalities related to written information

Another broad legal area to be considered is written announcements, notices, letter of information to parents, and press releases about critical incidents. They need to be written to meet legal requirements related to juveniles, particularly if a critical incident results from an offence. Likely no report can be published about the alleged offence to have been committed by a young person, in which the name of the young alleged perpetrator or the name of the young victim or witness is mentioned. Disclosures to any professional or person engaged in supervisory care of a young person, a representative of any school board or school, or any other educational or training institution should only be made if it is necessary to ensure the safety of staff, students, and other persons. All information should be handled and stored so that individual confidentiality is not compromised.

Legalities related to e-mail messages

The last area to consider is the use of e-mail messages. When using e-mail between schools or departments it is wise to remember that all e-mail messages are on record. Keep your communication confidential by not mentioning names, unless necessary for clear communication.

WHAT IS A CRISIS?

Crisis event versus crisis reaction

Fairchild stated that "a crisis is a period of psychological imbalance, which is experienced in the face of a hazardous or traumatizing event, which can neither be escaped nor solved with customary problem-solving behaviors," (1986). It is important to remember that any change creates stress. Depending on an individual's experience and coping skills, he or she will either successfully meet the challenges of change or become overwhelmed and be in an active crisis state. The individual experiencing the crisis may not be able to appropriately or effectively utilize his or her "usual" coping mechanisms, adding to the perceived helplessness in the current predicament (Trethowan, 2009). It can thus be said that a crisis is not necessarily an event, but an individual's perception of an event as being both dangerous and threatening. It is something the individual cannot succeed, or has not succeeded, in resolving, removing, avoiding, or controlling. On the other hand, a crisis resulting from specific situations is still a reality. These are referred to as **crisis events**. They tend to be uncontrollable, negative, and unexpected (Villarreal and Peterson, 2015).

Crisis intervention defined

Fairchild defines **crisis intervention** as the process whereby helpers attempt to restore psychological equilibrium by improving the individual's coping skills and offering new alternatives for handling the troubling situation (1986).

Origins of crises

Crises are an inevitable part of human existence occurring often in the lives of individuals and their families (Fairchild, 1986). The origins of crises fall into two categories, (Fairchild, 1986):

- situational or unanticipated
    - o material/environmental (fire or natural disaster)
    - o personal/physical (heart attack, fatal illness, loss of a limb)
    - o interpersonal/social (death of a loved one, divorce)
- transitional or anticipated
    - o universal (life cycle, normal transitions in human development)
    - o non-universal (changing jobs, retirement, moving)
    - o social origins
    - o violation of social norms (sexual assault, abuse, robbery, assault)

Avoiding a crisis

A crisis does not occur instantly; a process or series of developments must be present for a crisis or a crisis state to exist. At times, all that may be required is emotional support. Weeping openly and expressing sorrow are not signs that the individual is in an active crisis state. It is possible to exacerbate an existing situation and turn it into a critical incident by over-responding to the situation.

A potentially hazardous or traumatizing event is not by itself evidence that a crisis or crisis state exists, (Fairchild, 1986). Individuals responding to a critical incident must always guard against the possibility of creating a crisis when in fact one does not exist.

A crisis may be avoided if the following conditions occur:

- There is a hazardous event that intrudes on the lives of individuals.

- Individuals or groups perceive the event as important and threatening, thereby causing a state of tension and anxiety.

- Emotional reactions to the event occur.

- Individuals experiencing the tension rely on their customary coping behaviors to resolve the situation.

- These behaviors relieve the tension; thus, an internal state of psychological equilibrium is maintained.

- The hazardous event is resolved and emotional discomfort is alleviated.

- Individuals successfully deal with the event using familiar coping skills.

- Individuals remain unchanged with no prolonged behavioral or emotional disturbance.

The development of a crisis state

Fairchild also states that a crisis is an event that always combines both the potential for danger and an opportunity for growth (1986). Danger exists when the event creates a level of emotional discomfort that cannot be relieved using customary coping behaviors and skills. Growth exists when individuals seek help from friends or other persons and thus acquire new or more effective coping skills when dealing with a critical incident.

If the following sequence of events occurs, a **crisis state** exists:

- The hazardous event creates a level of emotional discomfort that cannot be relieved using customary coping skills.

- The event is important and threatening to individuals.

- Emotional reaction occurs in response to the incident.

- Normal coping behaviors are employed to deal with the incident.

- Normal coping behaviors are not effective.

- Individuals continue to employ ineffective coping behaviors to deal with the incident.

- Disorganization and psychological imbalance occur.

- Internal discomfort increases in intensity, both cognitive and emotional distortion occurs. Cognitive distortion refers to the inability to deal with reality, plan, and predict consequences. Emotional distortion refers to individual emotional reactivity, heightened feelings of helplessness, and the feeling that the situation is hopeless.

- Turmoil intensifies.

- The emotional discomfort is so debilitating that it takes the form of physical symptoms, such as insomnia, regressive behaviors, and withdrawal.

- A state of disorganization and psychological imbalance follows, and this reduces problem-solving capacity.

- Individuals are now in a state of active crisis because their present problem remains unresolved and the range of emotions that they are experiencing has risen to an unbearable degree.

- Individuals act to relieve the turmoil.

- The situation cannot be resolved, and individuals are in an active crisis state.

Duration of crises

Crises are limited in duration, lasting from two or three days to a few months. Most critical incidents tend to last approximately two days to a week. By the third day there are signs of routine and structure in the daily activities. In any event, there should be a follow-up scheduled approximately two weeks after the initial incident.

Consequences are long-term. They may be either adaptive (improved coping skills) or maladaptive (continued use of maladaptive coping skills). In the latter case, affected individuals have not learned any new skills to use the next time they are exposed to a traumatic event.

Outcomes of crises

Individuals exposed to a crisis will return to one of four possible outcomes. The outcome is dependent, in part, on whether the school has implemented an effective crisis plan, whether the affected students have participated in individual or group debriefings and defusing or group discussions, and whether they have accessed support at home.

- Individuals return to the pre-crisis state, but may experience post-traumatic stress disorder.

- Individuals return to the pre-crisis state but grow from the experience through acquiring new coping and problem-solving behaviors and skills.

- Individuals return to the pre-crisis state but do not grow from the experience or acquire new coping and problem-solving behaviors and skills.

- Individuals lapse into neurotic or psychotic patterns of behavior.

STEPS FOR SUCCESSFULLY MANAGING A CRISIS

If a traumatic event does develop, the immediate reaction and future consequences of the event on students and staff depend upon how quickly and effectively the school crisis team and staff respond to the situation. Immediate action is essential if staff is to maintain leadership and control throughout the incident. Successful management of a crisis tends to follow five specific steps, as follows.

(1) **Assess the crisis** - School helpers need to first determine whether individuals are, in fact, in a state of crisis. The school crisis team should determine the level of need and support. Care must be taken when looking for links to other individuals or situations. There is always the potential to develop a crisis state when in fact none exists.

(2) **Develop an intervention plan** - Only after helpers have a thorough understanding of the nature of the incident and its severity can they begin to formulate a plan of action. Crisis intervention should be short-term in nature. Maintenance strategies are most important. These are strategies that prevent the situation from deteriorating and the individuals' mental/physical health from declining further.

(3) **Implement the intervention plan** - This will require direction by school crisis team members. It is important to set achievable goals that can be obtained in small steps.

(4) **Evaluate and modify the plan** - Helpers should keep a record of the assessment information gathered. This should include working notes, a list of goals that have been identified for resolving the crisis, a list of the various activities and strategies that helpers have implemented, and a record of the effectiveness of the various strategies used.

(5) **Follow up post-crisis** - It is important to follow-up with individual assessment after the crisis has passed. This assures helpers that affected individuals have satisfactorily resolved their crises. This also assures individuals who had trouble coping that people care about them.

KEEPING RECORDS

With some students, the intervention plans may be verbal. It is also a good idea to keep accurate, written records when working with students in crisis. This is especially important today because schools are held increasingly liable for providing support services to children who are experiencing a crisis. Documentation provides some evidence that specific and appropriate intervention has taken place. It is easy to forget what has been said or suggested to a student or group, particularly during a crisis. Recording the date and nature of the incident is important for monitoring the anniversary date and individual responses at that time. Written records will also be helpful should there be legal concerns or questions about strategies and interventions implemented at the school. As well, written records and checklists provide an excellent source of information for reviewing and revising the school crisis plan.

Completing the forms

It is the responsibility of the principal in collaboration with the school crisis team to determine which forms, checklists, and logs may be used, modified, or deleted during a critical incident. Refer to forms developed for this purpose in Appendix 2.

Completion of the forms provides a record of specific strategies, procedures, and actions taken during a critical incident. They also provide documented evidence that may be beneficial to the school crisis team in the face of potential litigation.

Information that should be recorded includes:

- record of the assessment information gathered during the first interview

- names of the students contacted during the crisis

- list of goals and solutions students identified for resolving the crisis

- lists of all activities and strategies students and teachers will implement

- detailed information about the event and date that it occurred, date of a memorial service (if appropriate), identity of those most affected, as well as closest friends and relatives of the victim

- detailed records of the event, especially the exact date of the incident or death (in order to be prepared for changes in behavior on the anniversary of the incident)

- reviews of the effectiveness of all the strategies used (in order to make the task of tracking information easier)

File all completed forms and checklists for future reference. This information is evidence that action was taken at the school.

WHAT TO DO

Step 3: Mobilize the school crisis team – now!

TYPICAL SEQUENCE OF EVENTS AFTER A CRISIS

When a traumatic incident occurs, especially an event that involves a death or deaths, there usually is a predictable sequence of events that follows. The most traumatic time typically is the first day, with normalcy beginning to return around the third day. During these three days, anyone affected by the incident will be on an emotional roller coaster.

Day 1

This will be the most emotional day for staff and students. The needs of staff members should be met first so they can effectively meet student needs. During the first day defusing emotions, group discussions, classroom debriefings, student and staff counseling, setting up a student drop-in center, assigning hall monitors, and the preparation of an information letter to be sent to all parents are some of the more important activities. Staff meetings should occur before and after school so that school employees are kept completely informed about the crisis, the response taken by the school crisis team and the resources available to everyone. It is important to include all secretarial and custodial staff in these meetings. Identify students most at risk. Reduced structure and routine should be expected in most classrooms, especially the victim's or victims' classroom(s). Teachers should attempt to maintain some degree of structure and routine to help keep students focused on the activities and not on the crisis.

Day 2

The second day may not be as emotionally intense as the first. Student and staff counseling activities should continue. Students may continue to attend discussion groups and defusing sessions. Classroom activities may focus on helping students cope with and grieve the loss. The classroom teacher should start to deal with the personal effects of the deceased student, in the event of a student death. Additional students at risk should be identified. A staff debriefing should be conducted on this day or the next. Teachers should continue to maintain a degree of structure and routine in their classrooms.

Day 3

Some signs of closure should start to appear. Following a death or multiple deaths, there may be an increase in emotionality due to a pending memorial and the fact that some students may participate in a service for the deceased. If a death is due to suicide, a memorial is not recommended. If there is strong opposition by students to the school not participating in some form of memorial for the deceased, the service should be small. It is important not to glorify a suicide in any way because it may encourage copycat suicides. Student and staff counseling should continue. Make sure to assist students most at risk. There should be increased structure and routine in all classrooms. Schedule follow-up activities for approximately two weeks after the traumatic incident, with a second follow-up about six weeks after that. A crisis team debriefing should be conducted within the next week or two.

PERFORMING THE INITIAL ASSESSMENT

The onset of a crisis is a stressful time for all school staff. When the school crisis team is called into action at the school to deal with a critical incident, it enables teaching staff to concentrate on maintaining routine and stability for students. For a school crisis team to intervene effectively, helpers must first determine whether students are, in fact, in a crisis state.

The initial assessment should occur immediately and not over a period of days. This assessment should focus on immediate and identifiable concerns of students and must evaluate the risk to life, because there is potential danger to life when an individual is in an active state of crisis. Helpers must remember that the assessment is not something that is done to the individual, but is a counseling/interviewing process carried out with individuals through their active participation. This process may also include collaboration with significant others. Only after members of the school crisis team have conducted the initial assessment and understand the nature of the incident and its severity can they begin to develop an effective plan. Caution is advised when conducting the assessment because there is always the potential to develop a crisis state when in fact none exits.

> *Note - It cannot be presumed that individuals who are extremely emotionally upset are in a state of crisis. School helpers need to remember that the critical ingredient for a crisis state to exist is that in addition to being emotionally upset, individuals have exhausted their coping resources. They are at the point where they are experiencing severe emotional turmoil and can no longer cope effectively using their adaptive coping behaviors (Fairchild, 1986).*

Immediate crisis-team responsibilities

The school-based crisis team has numerous functions that are divided into three time frames: pre-crisis, crisis, and post-crisis. When developing, and adapting the crisis plan there are certain components and procedures that should be considered for each time frame. If they are followed, the crisis plan will operate much more effectively. As well, by following the plan in a systematic manner, you are less likely to forget a contact that should have been dealt with during the initial stages of the incident (Petersen and Straub, 1992). Immediate responsibilities/ steps for the school crisis team are presented below.

(1) Assemble the team and verify information.

(2) Contact the area superintendent.

(3) Adapt the plan to fit the current crisis.

(4) Meet with school staff and announce event.

(5) Request additional support from district/divisional crisis team, if necessary.

(6) Assign staff roles and responsibilities:

- o principal

- o counselors

- o teachers

- o school psychologist

- o secretary/school support staff

(7) Set up a student drop-in center (secondary schools).

(8) Set up a crisis center.

(9) Designate a person to whom all information will be sent and recorded.

(10) Assign hallway and washroom monitors.

(11) Assist or provide crisis counseling and debriefing.

(12) Write an information release for the media and an information letter to parents.

(13) Hire extra help for the front office.

(14) Hire substitute teachers familiar with the school.

(15) Notify the school bus company of the event.

(16) Gather information regarding the memorial (if the incident demands one).

(17) Schedule staff debriefing at later date, usually within the first three days.

Checking the facts

Many school systems have developed a liaison with their local police departments and medical examiner or coroner to ensure that they are contacted when an incident affecting the school occurs. This can be most helpful because it allows the school to put its crisis plan into effect promptly. In the face of serious trauma, rumors can run rampant. Establishing a line of communication with the police before an emergency arises assures that the facts are received and rumors are dispelled, thus alleviating anxiety and uncertainty. Initially establishing this line of communication may be difficult. Police departments are concerned with notifying the next of kin, as well as guarding against the premature release of any information that may be presented in court (Petersen and Straub, 1992). Once the initial tasks of checking the facts and assembling the crisis team have been completed, the team should concentrate on developing or adapting the crisis plan to the current situation. Before doing so verify the basic facts:

- Who was/were the victim(s)?
- How did they die? Accident? Suicide? Illness?
- When did they die?
- Where did they die?
- Did anyone witness the death(s)? Who?
- Who were close friends of the victim(s)?
- How was/were the death(s) discovered? By whom?
- Does the victim (or victims) have siblings or relatives attending different schools?

Adapting the plan to fit the crisis

The crisis team members should have a sound understanding of the various crisis intervention techniques in order that they make informed decisions and avoid complicating the situation further. They may be required to alter or modify their procedures and strategies, depending on the nature and scope of the situation. The goal of any crisis intervention is to prevent further trauma to children and prevent post-traumatic stress disorder. When adapting the intervention plan consider these points.

How will the announcement be made?

- Can you tell your school staff first?
- Is this a school wide crisis?
- Do you need to request additional support from the district/division?
- Can you announce the event in such a way that it does not become sensationalized?
- Will rumors and speculation result because of the way the announcement is made?
- How do you expect the staff, students, and the parents to react to the news?
- Who should be notified within your school system?
- Should a statement be posted on the school's website?

If a death has occurred, will a memorial service be held?

- How widespread is the effect of this tragedy on your students?
- Is this an incident that should be memorialized at the school?
- Will the service be open to the public, the press, or parents?
- Set the date, time, and location of any school memorial service.
- Will the location accommodate the number of people projected to attend?

- Are the parents of the deceased supportive of a school memorial service?
- Are there any special religious considerations that must be observed?

Does the school have any legal responsibility?

- How will you inform parents?
- Has an information letter for parents been prepared?
- What supports, if any will you provide for parents?
- Are students or staff likely to face bouts of depression? How will you prepare them?
- Who can you contact from your school board or community for assistance?

How will you address the media?

- Who is your spokesperson? This should be the principal, or another person as pre-determined through divisional/district policy.
- Is this incident likely to draw national attention?
- Has a written statement for the press been prepared?
- Has a time and a location been set to meet with the media?

How much staff support is needed?

- Is it necessary to provide counseling for staff?
- Who will provide this faculty support?
- Have a time and location been established to meet with the staff after the school day?
- Is employment assistance program counseling available to staff?

CONTACTING SCHOOL STAFF

Staff notification depends a great deal upon when the news of the event breaks. If possible, sensitive information should be delivered in person. Establishing a telephone contact tree, whereby each staff member has three names to call provides a pre-established avenue of communication (Petersen and Straub, 1992). When time allows, this method can be used to arrange a staff meeting before school. Staff members can then be personally informed of the tragedy when they are together at the meeting (for example, before classes begin in the morning). This approach provides the greatest support and it most effectively reduces rumors. If time does not allow a staff meeting before school, then, the news of the event can be given directly to the staff through the telephone tree. If the crisis occurs during the instructional day, the principal may consider calling the crisis team to the office and then sending members back to systematically inform their colleagues. The principal might speak to the teachers individually and/or send a critical incident alert form to each teacher informing them of the basic facts of the incident. Informing the staff first helps to maintain maximum control over the reaction of staff and students because the information given is accurate and consistent. Teachers should also have an opportunity to release some of their own grief and offer comfort to each other before they begin to support students and parents.

It is important to schedule another meeting with the staff at the end of the day after the students have left, to discuss the events and reactions which occurred during the day and to inform them of what might be expected the following day. Giving support to so many children for an entire day is very draining. Teachers also create emotional bonds with their students and are thereby affected by the loss. Allow time to discuss ways they might recover from the crisis before facing the students again the next day. Have the counselor or school psychologist brief teachers on what to expect of the students during the next few weeks and explain how the teachers can help. The support you provide for your staff now will enhance cohesion amongst the student body as well.

Using a telephone contact tree

Extend a chart like the one below far enough to fill in the names and telephone numbers of all school staff members. Each person then has three people to phone when he or she receives a call about a crisis. Distribute to all staff and post in staff room.

Name: _____
#: _____

Name: _____
#: _____

Name: _____
#: _____

Name: _____
#: _____

Name: _____
#: _____

Name: _____
#: _____

Name: _____
#: _____

Name: _____
#: _____

Name: _____
#: _____

Name: _____
#: _____

Name: _____
#: _____

Name: _____
#: _____

Name: _____
#: _____

Name: _____
#: _____

Name: _____
#: _____

Name: _____
#: _____

Name: _____
#: _____

Name: _____
#: _____

Name: _____
#: _____

Name: _____
#: _____

Name: _____
#: _____

Adapted from Petersen, S., and Straub, R.L. (1992)

MAKING THE ANNOUNCEMENT IN SCHOOL

The announcement to staff and students must convey the facts of the incident in a sensitive and compassionate manner. Keep in mind the fight-or-flight response to trauma. The announcement should be made in a way that will contain these intense emotional reactions. If there are individuals known to be especially close to the victim, the news should be delivered in private. The public-address system should not be used to announce the death of a student. Teachers should make this announcement in their classrooms. Only when a loss is school-wide should use of the public-address system be considered. Sample announcements are provided below, (Petersen and Straub, 1992).

Sample Announcements

In classroom (loss related to an individual child)

_____ will not be in school today. _____'s father was killed in a vehicle accident last night. A truck struck his car on the highway.

_____ will be very sad for a long time. Perhaps we can discuss some ways that _____ might be feeling and how we can all help him/her.

In classroom (school-wide loss)

We have something very sad to tell you today.

_____ was driving home in the rain last night. His/her car swerved into an oncoming lane, was struck by another car and went off the road.

_____ died in the crash. It was sudden and he/she did not suffer.

Over public address system (school-wide loss)

Our school has suffered a great, great loss.

_____ the science teacher, has been ill with cancer for many months now. We just received word that his/her suffering has come to an end and he/she has died. We will be commemorating _____'s contributions to our school community. Now, I'd like each class to discuss the ways they would like to commemorate the life work of _____.

In classroom (declared suicide)

We are sad to announce that _____ took his/her life last night. His/her family will make memorial service arrangements. Counseling will be provided for those who wish to speak with a counselor.

It is always a shock when we hear of someone taking his or her own life. Let's cancel work this morning to discuss this.

In classroom (undeclared suicide or fact has not been made public)

_____ died last night of a gunshot wound. He/she apparently had a gun in his/her hand when it fired. Counseling will be provided for those who wish to speak with someone. When an unexpected incident such as this occurs, it helps to discuss it. Regular class work will be canceled to allow time for discussion.

STAFF ROLES AND RESPONSIBILITIES

The school crisis team leader (this should be the principal), should inform the all staff members about their responsibilities during a crisis. This action alone reduces much of the staff anxiety and instills in them the confidence needed to support the students. Discussing staff responsibilities prior to a crisis allows time for expression of dissension and helps to guarantee that the follow-through the team has decided upon will take place during an actual crisis.

Below are suggested roles and responsibilities, as adapted from Petersen and Straub (1992).

Principal

- Contact the area superintendent.
- Verify the accuracy of the information from the police.
- Activate the school crisis team.
- Meet with staff to announce the event before school starts.
- Determine if support is needed from the district/division.
- Determine if additional resources are needed.
- Remain highly visible.
- Set the tone and direction.
- Chair the crisis team.
- Meet with staff after school.
- Contact other schools if necessary.
- Set time and location to meet with the media. Prepare a statement for the media.
- Prepare an information letter to be sent to all parents.
- State clear procedures for secretarial staff responding to calls or requests from parents, media, or others.
- If appropriate, call the clergy to be available for counseling.

- Cancel scheduled activities.
- Seek additional secretarial support.

Counselor

- Provide counseling services for students.
- Plan the logistics of counseling.
- Lead debriefings, defusing sessions, and group discussions.
- Establish the student drop-in center.
- Coordinate all counseling activities in the school.
- Communicate with teaching staff and principal.
- Seek additional counseling support.
- Provide information to parents.
- Identify students most at risk.

Teachers

- Announce the event to the students in their classrooms.
- Lead class discussions/debriefings.
- Identify students in need of counseling.
- Allow students to go to the drop-in center.
- Identify those students most likely to need support (e.g., close relatives, friends of victim).
- Generate activities to reduce the impact of trauma.
- Structure and shorten assignments.
- Postpone testing.
- Request additional support, if needed.
- Deal with the victim's personal belongings.
- Network with colleagues for support.
- Monitor own needs.
- Maintain structure and routine in the classroom.

Secretary

- Maintain a telephone log of all calls from parents, media, and other schools about the event.
- Give only approved information as determined by the crisis response team; refer to official spokesperson if one is appointed.
- Type prepared information letters to parents.
- Escort parents who arrive at the school to the reception area.
- Ensure parents and staff have access to coffee, tea, and food.
- Attend all meetings; record minutes as advised by principal.
- Contact external agencies as advised.
- Meet all media personnel at front door and escort to and from scheduled meetings.
- Maintain a student sign in/out log.
- Contact parents as directed by the principal.
- Maintain record of all individuals coming in to the school.
- Identify and refer students at risk.
- Take time for yourself.

School psychologists

- Provide support and counseling to staff.
- Conduct student counseling as directed.
- Lead debriefings, defusing sessions, and group discussions when requested.
- Monitor students in hallways and other unsupervised areas.
- Assist the principal with letter to parents if requested.
- Provide information (post-traumatic stress disorder/debriefings) to students and staff.
- Meet with concerned parents if requested.

Support staff

- Follow the crisis intervention plan.
- Attend all staff meetings.
- Request support when needed.
- Identify and refer students at risk.
- Maintain professionalism.

- Respect confidentiality.
- Know who is in the building.

CLASSROOM ACTIVITIES

Teachers did not choose education as a career so that they might deal with crisis issues. They will need some reassurance that they can handle the students and the critical incident, and that they are doing a good job. Suggestions for age-appropriate classroom activities follow in the next sections and can be reviewed when staff members discuss their responsibilities.

Preschool activities

Creative classroom activities may be helpful to teachers seeking ways to deal with the stress and tension of a crisis and its effects on students. The following activities are vehicles for expression and discussion for students, and are important steps in helping them handle the stress they are experiencing. You can use these activities to stimulate your own ideas and adapt them to meet both your students' needs and your teaching style (Johnson, 1993).

- Make available toys that encourage play enactment of the child's concerns. Such toys might include airplanes, helicopters, toy police officers, rescue trucks, ambulances, building blocks, puppets, or dolls. Playing with these toys allows the child to ventilate feelings about what is occurring or has already occurred.

- Children need lots of physical contact during times of stress to help them re-establish their sense of security. Introduce structured games that involve physical touching among children.

- Provide extra amounts of drinks and finger foods in small portions. This is a concrete way of supplying the emotional and physical nourishment children need in times of stress. Oral satisfaction is especially necessary because children tend to exhibit more regressive behaviors in response to feelings that threaten their survival or security.

- Have the children make a mural, using topics related to what is happening in the world and in their community. This is recommended for small groups, with discussion afterwards facilitated by the teacher or another skilled adult.

- Have the children draw individual pictures about the crisis and then discuss the pictures in small groups. This activity allows children to vent their experiences and to discover that others share their fears.

- Make a group collage, and discuss what the collage represents, how it was made, and the feelings it evokes.

Helper's response to preschool/kindergarten students

Goal:
- Re-establish trust and security.

30

- Re-establish self-control and autonomy.

Method:

- Provide physical comforts (e.g. warm milk, cuddling or holding the child, food).

- Re-establish structure and routines.

- Assure and provide adult protection.

- Let parents know that it is all right for the child to temporarily sleep in the parents' room.

- Help the child draw, act out, and discuss incident.

- Clarify event, misconceptions, and misunderstandings.

- Be calm.

Elementary school activities

- For younger children, make toys available that encourage play to express concerns, fears, and observations. These toys might include ambulances, planes, tanks, helicopters, toy police officers, rescue vehicles, toy soldiers, building blocks, and dolls. Play with puppets can provide ways for older children, as well as younger children, to ventilate their feelings (Johnson, 1993).

- Help or encourage children to develop skits or puppet shows about what happened during the crisis. Encourage them to include anything positive about the experience as well as frightening or disconcerting aspects.

- Have the children create short stories about the crisis and how it was managed. These stories can be either written or dictated to an adult, depending on the age of the child.

- Have the children draw pictures and discuss them in relation to the crisis. It is important that the group discussion end on a positive note.

- Stimulate group discussion about the crisis and its consequences by showing your own feelings or fears. It is very important to legitimize children's feelings and to help them feel less isolated. It is equally important to give them a sense of structure, balance, and control over their own activities and life.

Have the children brainstorm their own ways of handling their concerns. Encourage them to discuss the results with their parents.

Encourage class activities in which the children can organize and build projects, such as scrapbooks, to give them a sense of mastery and ability to organize what seems to be chaotic and confusing.

In small groups, encourage children to talk about their feelings about the crisis (should be facilitated by an adult) (Center for Mental Health in Schools at UCLA, 2008).

Helper's response to elementary students

Goal:

- Bolster self-esteem.
- Relieve guilt.
- Re-establish productivity.
- Provide reassurances of safety.

Method:

- Encourage the expression of thoughts and feelings.
- Validate the normalcy of student reactions.
- Re-establish structure and routines.
- Lessen requirements for optimal performance.
- Reinforce age-appropriate behavior.
- Provide structure as behavior indicates.
- Allow expression of feelings of responsibility; clarify misconceptions.

Junior/senior high school activities

The following suggestions could be carried out within specific courses at the school. Teachers are encouraged to expand these suggestions to fit the students' needs and the teachers' individual styles (Johnson, 1993).

- Conduct a group discussion of the students' experiences concerning the crisis and the events surrounding it. This is particularly important to adolescents because they need the opportunity to vent as well as to normalize the extreme emotions that arise. A good way to stimulate such a discussion is to share your personal reactions. This modeling will provide the students with an example of how to share their feelings and contribute to the discussion. The students may need considerable reassurance that even extreme emotions and "crazy" thoughts are normal under these circumstances. It is important to end the discussions on a positive note. Such discussions are appropriate for any course of study because they can hasten the return to more normal functioning.

- Conduct a class discussion or support a class project on how students might involve themselves in activities related to managing the crisis. This might include support groups, rallies, and assistance to family members. It is important to help students develop concrete, realistic ways to assist or be involved. This helps them to overcome the feelings of helplessness, frustration, and guilt, common reactions to these situations.

- Introduce classroom activities that relate the crisis and its consequences to the course of study. This can be an effective way to help students integrate their own experiences or observations while providing specific learning experiences. When performing these activities, it is important to allow time for students to discuss the feelings stimulated by the projects or the other issues covered.

Helper's response to junior/senior high students

Goal:

- Inoculate against secondary reactions.
- Emphasize stress management.
- Facilitate identity development.
- Reaffirm life direction.

Method:

- Encourage discussion and expression.
- Validate the normalcy of student reactions.
- Re-establish structure and routines.
- Lessen requirements for optimal performance.
- Provide opportunity for positive action.
- Provide monitoring and guidance.
- Provide conceptualization of the incident, reactions, and situation.

TEACHER DO'S AND DON'TS

During a critical incident, many teachers are concerned about what they should say and do in the classroom. Not knowing what to say or do is often the cause of considerable stress and anxiety for the teacher. Clayton provides several suggestions, which are listed below (Crisis Intervention Guide, 1994).

Do

- Feel comfortable in asking for help because you do not have to handle the experience alone.
- Use the correct, concrete terminology. Avoid using such euphemisms as "gone to sleep, long journey" etc.
- Use age appropriate language.
- Tell the truth about the incident without unnecessary details.
- Development an environment in which students feel safe to discuss and question.
- Give honest answers.
- Listen and empathize.
- Remember to share your own feelings.
- Allow your students to express as much grief as they are willing to share with you.

- Allow students to release strong feelings of anger and bitterness about what they are feeling.

- Remember to say, "I don't know" if that is the case.

- Organize activities that will allow students to tangibly express their grief.

- Be flexible about your normal classroom routine.

- Note any student who is having significant difficulty coping and report to the counselor and parents.

- Share with the class the opportunity to collect the deceased's belongings.

- Don't forget to carefully edit all messages, letters, and cards sent by students to a grieving family for appropriateness.

Don't

- Don't immediately remove all evidence of a deceased student's or teacher's presence in the classroom.

- Do not deal in rumors or speculation. If asked personal, sensitive, or embarrassing questions about the death, stick to the facts only. Do not get into descriptive or gory details about the death.

- Don't use philosophical, religious, or sentimental references.

- Don't make individual participation in classroom discussions mandatory.

- Don't lecture, moralize, or cast judgment.

- Don't link suffering and death with guilt, punishment, and sin.

- Don't expect adult responses from students, even teenagers.

- Don't ridicule or belittle any questions.

- Don't force others to look for something positive in the tragedy.

- Don't say, "I know how you feel."

- Don't force a regular day on grieving students.

WHAT TO DO

Step 4: Deal with the media and address parents' concerns

BE PROACTIVE – CONTACT PARENTS AND THE MEDIA

We assume that the principal will be the one responsible for dealing with the media (print, radio, television, etc.) In some districts/divisions, assigned communication staff controls the release of information and provide general information to the press about the event and actions taken by the district/division.

It is important to make sure every team member is familiar with all aspects of the school/district's media relations policies (Jimerson et al., 2005). It will also be helpful to have a team member reviewing media reports to ensure consistent and accurate media reporting and the release of prompt reactionary press releases by the official liaison (Jimerson et al., 2005).

Principals are responsible for dealing with parents, but may choose to seek support from district/divisional communication staff. The principal is also responsible for keeping all staff informed of the facts as they become available. Staff must understand the importance of squelching rumors.

During a crisis, thinking of media as a kind of "middle-man"

The wise principal will be prepared for public scrutiny. Nickerson et al. (2006) recommend that whoever oversees media contact and information sharing should build positive and productive relationships with both broadcast and print media. Once you have developed a good working relationship with the press, you are in a much stronger position. The media can then become an extension of your communication from the school. This can work to the school's advantage in that the press can help spread the word to the community as

Principals consistently report that dealing with the media is the most difficult part of handling a crisis (Johnson, 1993). The responsibility to protect students and to respond to community's concerns is enormous. This area, more than any other, requires forethought and preparation.

Do not delegate the task of speaking with journalists. The community sees the principal as overseeing the school and responsible for the actions taken or avoided. As the visible leader of the school, the principal must speak to the press and determine the limits of journalists' involvement at the school. This can be achieved by submitting information about specific programs, successes and awards achieved at your school, and other human interest stories. Principals should remember that citizens have a right to know what is happening at the school.

Accommodating differences between your agenda and the agenda of the media

Reporters see their role as being responsible for bringing this important information to the public. Do your best to help them fulfill this role. If you encounter a reporter who is either insensitive to the situation or tends to distort what you say, give that person minimal information. Do not attempt to exclude them from a story. This will make things worse.

When asked questions by reporters, answer without volunteering information. You can give different levels of information. Also, avoid the response "no comment." This tends to suggest that there may be an attempt to hide something. The "no comment" approach will not eliminate all the difficulties you may encounter with the press during an incident (Petersen and Straub, 1992).

SETTING LIMITS FOR MEDIA ACCESS

Principals have the right to determine who is allowed on school property and to which areas of the school they have access. Principals are advised to use this right proactively by setting limits for the media. This means that during the initial call or contact with the media inform them as to where, when, and for how long you will meet with them. By following this procedure, you will help maintain the necessary order, establish your authority, and reduce stress to students.

To protect students and staff while reporters are present, an interview site should be chosen that is away from the main area of student activity. The meeting itself does not have to be long. It should be long enough to deliver the prepared statement followed by a short question period. At this time, no teachers or students should be available for interviews and no members of the media should be admitted beyond the meeting area.

When reporters arrive, have a staff member familiar with the guidelines accompany them to the meeting location and back to the front door after the meeting is over. Do not leave reporters unescorted while on school property. It is wise to clearly state all restrictions placed on the media while on school property when scheduling the first meeting. Ensure that members of the media understand and agree to these restrictions.

Ground rules around interviewing on school property

The principal has the right to deny the media interviews with teachers on school property. Teachers have the right to deny an interview at any time or place. No staff or faculty member is required to be interviewed by the media.

If the media is attempting to interview a teacher, the principal must obtain the teacher's permission to be interviewed, and then grant them permission to be interviewed while on school property.

36

If a reporter is attempting to interview a student, the principal must grant permission and the student must be willing to be interviewed. Parental permission should be sought. Some parents may choose not to have their children interviewed by the media.

GUIDELINES FOR COMMUNICATING WITH THE MEDIA

- Develop a written statement for the media.

- Develop a message to be given over the telephone and assign people to handle the phones.

- Appoint a spokesperson to deal with the media; this should be the principal.

- Set a time and location to meet with the media, and any follow-up meetings, in advance.

- Appoint a staff person to escort media to and from any meeting at the school. Do not leave the media unescorted while on school property.

- Be proactive with the press; contact the media before they contact you.

- State any restrictions imposed on reporters while on school property. Allow no photographs, no student interviews, no teacher interviews unless approved by the principal and teacher, etc.

- Never try to speak to the media "off the record."

- Stress positive action taken by your school; provide periodic updates.

- Maintain confidentiality where necessary.

- Stress services available to students.

- Do not refuse to speak with the press.

- Announce changes made after the incident.

Preparing a written statement

Prior to meeting with the media have a written statement prepared. Prepare this statement with input from your crisis team. State only the facts and avoid speculation. Once the facts have been reported, present the positive actions the school is taking to help students deal with the incident. This is also a good time to make community announcements relating to events such as a memorial service, parent meetings, and follow-up activities for students. All statements must be truthful; false statements will eventually come to the surface. A perspective that the school is attempting to cover up important facts or information will cause trouble. Do not issue disclaimers of responsibility until all facts are known. The school needs to be dealing with the problem, not attempting to abdicate responsibility. The principal should remind the media of the consequences of sensationalizing a suicide if that is the situation at hand. The principal is the most appropriate person to prepare and issue the official statement at the school. Though the local or area superintendent oversees schools, it is the principal who is seen by the community as being ultimately responsible for the school.

Sample announcements to the media

Examples of announcements that may be made by the principal to the media are included below. The communications officer may make similar announcements to the media, though the focus should be limited to information about the departmental response to the affected school and school crisis team. It would be beneficial to link announcements with social media such as the school's Twitter account. This is because many people find out local news through social media platforms thanks to trend focused news dissemination.

Example 1

Our third-grade students were on a field trip when their school bus was involved in an accident on the _____ highway. Rescue is on the scene, transporting students to the hospital. Our vice-principal is also at the scene of the accident now. We have established a special hotline for parents to call for more information. The number is _____.

Our crisis team has gone into action, helping the staff and students. More information will be released as we receive it.

Important points made in this example are:

- the preparedness of the school for incidents of this nature
- access to information for the parents
- responsible, immediate action taken by a powerful school representative at the scene
- support already provided for students at the school

Example 2

A fight involving two eleventh-grade students occurred a half block from school at 7 P.M. last evening. The incident resulted in the fatal shooting of one of our students. Police are investigating and no more is known at this time. Our school's crisis plan went into action immediately following the incident and these are the actions already taken:

Our crisis committee met last night. A parent hotline has been established; the number is _____.

Resources have been called in to assist our recovery.

Counseling for students will be provided.

Review and reinforcement of our school violence policy is underway.

Important points made in this example include the following:

- There is an expression of loss.
- The incident is coupled with a statement about the violence policy thereby portraying the school as a positive force within the community.

- Access to information is made available immediately for concerned parents, thus demonstrating the forthrightness of the principal and the ability of the school staff to handle emergencies.

Example 3

It is with great sadness that the staff and students have learned today of the death of one of our students, John Doe.

John came to the school three years ago and was a student in the sixth-grade class. He was a conscientious student who worked hard.

Our heartfelt sympathies go out to his parents and the other members of his family.

He was a fine young man and will be greatly missed.

DEALING WITH PARENTS AT THE SCHOOL

During a crisis, it is not unusual to have anxious parents come to the school. These are concerned parents who are worried about their child's emotional and physical wellbeing. Some parents fear that their child may be negatively influenced by the death of a peer, especially in the case of a suicide, or that their child may not be able to cope with the death. It is important to assure these parents that their children are safe and that appropriate measures are being taken immediately to prevent further trauma due to the critical event.

When parents arrive at the school they should be taken to a predetermined location in the school where they have access to coffee/tea and, if available, light refreshments. Efforts should be made to prevent parents from wandering about the school. If parents wish to withdraw their child from the school, they should not be sent to the classroom to retrieve the child; instead a staff member responsible for monitoring parents should do this. The parent should remain in the predetermined location while the staff member retrieves their child.

When parents are at the school, they should be given an opportunity to speak with one of the crisis team members who can answer questions. Often parents do not know what to say or do after their child has been involved in or exposed to a critical incident. In response to this need, a crisis team member should schedule time after school to meet with parents. During this meeting suggestions and information should be provided to parents so they can assist their children to cope more effectively with the critical incident.

PREPARING AN INFORMATION LETTER TO PARENTS

Since many parents will have concerns about their children and their ability to deal effectively with the critical incident, an information letter is prepared at the school by the principal and sent home with every child in the school. The principal is the most appropriate and influential person to write the information letter to parents.

The letter outlines the nature of the situation without violating confidentiality. It should also detail steps taken, services offered at the school for students and an acknowledgement of loss (if a death is involved). The back of the letter can list the emotional, behavioral, and cognitive signs of stress, as well as strategies that parents may take to help their children cope with the incident. Parents are told these signs are a normal reaction to a traumatic event. It is important to contact the parents of any students who are having a difficult time coping with the death.

There are seven important points made in both letters. These points should be included in all such letters.

- statement of positive characteristics of the student

- immediate response by the school

- what students have been told about the incident

- services available to students

- availability of specialists at the school to answer questions from parents

- expression of loss and condolences

- specific information about grief and coping

Example 1

May 17, 2016

Dear parents and guardians:

This morning we received news that the body of Tom Smith was found Wednesday evening in a rocky area near the ski hill. He has been missing since January 21, 2016. Tom had been a student at our school for the past three years. He was a quiet, conscientious student with a keen interest in sports. Tom was well liked by his peers and teachers.

Our school responded this morning by informing students of the sad news. We arranged for counseling within the school. Students were given the opportunity to attend a debriefing session conducted by our counselors. A counseling area has been established in the school and students with concerns have been encouraged to attend. We are pleased with the level of support offered by the community, staff, department of education, and fellow students.

Counseling services will continue through this week and as needed thereafter. We have also included suggestions, which you may find helpful, for assisting your child in coping with Tom's death.

If you have questions about your child's response to the news of Tom's death, please call _____, our school counselor, or _____, principal, at _____.

Our condolences are extended to Tom's family, friends, and members of the school community as they deal with his untimely death.

Yours sincerely,

Principal

Example 2

Dear Parents/Guardians:

On Saturday, we received news that one of our students, Jane Doe, had been involved in a fatal vehicle accident. The accident occurred on Friday evening at _____. We understand that there was prompt response by the police, ambulance, and medical services. Jane passed away en route to the hospital. She was actively involved in our student council and a member of our basketball team. Jane was a very friendly and popular student at our school, well-liked by her peers and teachers. Jane will be greatly missed.

Our school responded on Sunday with the implementation of our crisis plan. Teachers were contacted and our department school psychologist arrived. The school was open on Monday for student counseling and support. We were pleased with the turnout and way students were supporting one another.

Today at the school students were informed about the facts related to the accident and were provided with opportunities to discuss their feelings and strategies related to ways of coping with their loss. A counseling area has been established in the school library and students who have expressed the need to talk or receive support have been encouraged to attend. We are pleased with the level of support offered by the community, staff, department of education, and fellow students.

Counseling services will continue through to Thursday afternoon and as needed thereafter. Our school psychologist is expected to return to _____ next Monday through Wednesday. We have also included suggestions, on the back of this letter, which you may find helpful in assisting your child in coping with Jane's death.

If you have questions about your child's response to the news of Jane's death, please call our counselor or myself at _____.

Our condolences are extended to the family, friends, and members of the school community as they deal with Jane's untimely death.

Yours sincerely,

Principal

Sample content for reverse side of information letter

Helping children work through their grief:

- *Be aware of your own feelings about loss in general, and about children and death.*
- *Help them grieve by sharing information, acknowledging reactions and feelings, and providing opportunities for expression.*
- *Acknowledge their pain; don't overprotect or hurry them.*

- *Be comfortable to sit and listen; your behavior and attitude is more important than words.*

- *Provide information about the grief process.*

- *Maintain structure and routine while allowing some flexibility for needs; involve children in decisions.*

- *Offer opportunities for rituals and times to remember the person who has died.*

- *If they are not talking to you, find out if they have other supports: teachers, friends, neighbors, or relatives.*

- *If you have questions or concerns, consult with a grief counselor, art or play therapist, or child psychologist.*

Characteristics of adolescent grief:

- *Their initial response may include shock, numbness, and/or disbelief.*

- *They may next feel helpless and frightened, or may try to "carry on."*

- *They may feel conflict between childlike needs and adult-like expectations.*

- *Anger (already present in a major way in teens) is now focused towards death.*

- *They may begin to act out their feelings.*

- *They may idealize the dead person.*

- *They may experience guilt and self-blame.*

- *They may experience delayed mourning.*

- *They may adopt clinging to mannerisms, ideas, and behaviors of the person who has died.*

- *They may experience fear of renewed closeness.*

- *They may behave in negative ways to elicit care from others.*

Emergency agencies and telephone numbers:

- *crisis line*

- *social worker*

- *poison control*

- *physician*

- *police*

- *clergy*

HOW PARENTS CAN HELP CHILDREN COPE

Grieving children will need continued support at home. Even though they may have talked extensively with peers, teachers, and counselors at school they will have questions and concerns that will come up while they are at home. Parents can help their children by following the suggestions listed below.

Helpful ACTIONS by parents

- Talk with your child and provide clear and simple answers to his or her questions.
- Talk about your own feelings; this modeling validates the child's own emotions.
- Listen to your child. Remember that you cannot talk and listen at the same time.
- Provide reassurance to your child that things will be all right.
- Provide physical comfort.
- Make sure that your child sleeps sufficiently, eats well, and exercises.
- Take the time to tuck your child in bed at night.
- If needed, repeat information and reassurances to your child.
- Make time to play with your child. This helps to relieve tension.
- If your child has a security blanket or toy, let them rely on it more than usual.

Helpful REACTIONS by parents

- Be aware of your own feelings about loss in general, and death, in particular.
- Help your children grieve by sharing information, acknowledging reactions and feelings, providing opportunities for expression.
- Acknowledge their pain; don't overprotect or hurry them.
- Be comfortable to sit and listen; your behavior and attitude are more important than words.
- Provide information about the grief process.
- Maintain structure and routine while allowing some flexibility for needs; involve youth in decisions.
- Offer opportunities for rituals and times to remember the person who has died.
- If they are not talking to you, find out if they have other supports: teachers, friends, neighbors, relatives.
- If you have questions or concerns, consult with the school counselor, or a counselor at a local hospice.

Helping teenagers deal with grief

Listed below are some common ways in which teenaged children deal with death or grief. Parents may find this information useful.

- Youth at this age can understand the permanence of death and initially respond with shock, disbelief, or numbness.

- They may have difficulty concentrating; may feel helpless and frightened; may be anxious.

- They may begin to act out feelings; may behave in negative ways to elicit care from others.

- They may exhibit physical symptoms such as headaches; loss of appetite or overeating; rashes, and other vague pains.

- They may feel conflict between child-like needs and adult-like expectations.

- Their "usual" teenager anger may now become focused on death.

- They may feel guilt and self-blame, especially if they remember a negative interaction with the deceased individual.

- They may experience delayed mourning (and if this symptom occurs later, consider the possibility that it may be related to an earlier loss).

- They may cling to mannerisms (ideas and behaviors) of the person who has died.

- They may revert to "younger," more dependent behavior.

**WHAT
TO DO**

Step 5: Reduce traumatic stress – offer crisis counseling

ESTABLISHING A STUDENT DROP-IN CENTER

When a traumatic incident involving junior/senior high students develops one of the first strategies for dealing with many students is to establish a student drop-in center in the school. The center is an area in the school where students can go to receive support and help in dealing with the incident. Two or more staff members should monitor the center. The structure at the center is informal and students are encouraged to talk among themselves. The center should remain set up for two or three days. It is important not to refer to the center as a counseling center, as this may have negative connotations to some students. When establishing a center, consider the following points, as outlined by a small rural community school district:

- Designate the library or another large classroom as the student drop-in center.

- Ensure that all students and staff know where the center is located.

- Assign at least two counselors or team members to the center. They will provide support and assistance to students as needed.

- If possible have coffee, tea, and juice available.

- Encourage students to express their feelings about the loss.

- Provide an atmosphere that is non-judgmental. Remember that students need someone who is willing to listen to them.

- Review the facts of the incident and remember to point out that the students are in no way responsible for what has happened, especially if the critical incident is a suicide. Close friends of the victim may feel they are responsible for the death or could have prevented it. Discuss feelings of survivor guilt associated with the incident.

- Encourage students to provide mutual support to each other.

- Keep large groups of students from forming as this may contribute to hysteria. Students tend to feed off the emotions of each other. If a large group begins to form, ensure that one of the counselors or crisis team members is in the group.

- Help students identify what resources they will use to cope with the situation.

- Remember to rotate staff members assigned to the center.

- Remind all teachers that any student may attend the center.

MONITORING AREAS WHERE STUDENTS TEND TO GATHER

Areas of the school that should be monitored include all hallways and washrooms. These are areas where students tend to gather. Students should not be left to roam about the school or gather in unsupervised areas. The emotional state of some individuals may cause them to become destructive and there is potential for damage to school property. Most often this damage is inflicted in response to the grief and anger experienced by individuals close to the victim. Other students not affected by the incident may, in fact, be influenced by the emotionality of the affected individuals in these areas of congregation. Thus, it is important to appoint staff to monitor these areas.

MONITORING AND ASSESSING AFFECTED INDIVIDUALS

During a critical incident, it is important to assess an individual's overall functioning. Observe and listen to the person. Present problems during a discussion to determine ability to problem-solve, and evaluate general stability. Ability to make changes and deal with the world each day is vital to how the individual copes and deals with crisis-related hurdles. It is not unusual for individuals to be slightly disoriented and confused. Some individuals may be either moderately or seriously impaired. Signs of moderate/severe impairment during and after the incident follow.

Signs of moderately impaired functioning during an incident

This information has been adapted from work completed by Johnson (1993).

Cognitive signs

- confusion

- difficulty solving problems

- trouble prioritizing

- time distortions

- memory loss

- anomie (disorientation/alienation caused by the perceived absence of social/emotional support)

Physical signs

- headache

- heart palpitations

- muffled hearing

- nausea

- cramps

- profuse sweating

- faintness

- rapid breathing

Emotional signs

- fear

- anxiety

- anger

- irritability

- frustration

Behavioral signs

- lethargy

- aimless wandering

- dejection

- hysteria

- memory problems

- hyperactivity

Signs of moderately impaired functioning after an incident

Cognitive signs

- fear of "going crazy"
- preoccupation with incident
- orientation toward past
- denial of importance of event
- problems concentrating

Physical signs

- fatigue
- psychosomatic problems

- increased illness
- physical concerns

Emotional signs

- depression
- grief
- numbness
- resentment/rage
- guilt
- fear of reoccurrence
- phobic reactions

Behavioral signs

- substance abuse
- self-destructive behavior
- sudden lifestyle changes
- social withdrawal
- sleep disorders
- compulsive talking
- avoidance behavior
- problems at work or school
- family problems
- flashbacks, nightmares

Signs of seriously impaired functioning during/after an incident

It is important to remember that a crisis creates disturbances in various areas (e.g. cognition, emotion, and behavior). These disturbances should be expected and are usually transitory in nature, but when these disturbances go to an extreme they impair individual functioning. When functioning is impaired the individual's ability to make rational decisions may be seriously impaired. The person will apply a solution or problem-focused approach to dealing with the crisis. Below are signs of serious impairment during and after a critical incident.

Individuals should be referred for an immediate psychiatric assessment when there are signs and symptoms of serious impairment. This is an indication that the individual is having difficulty functioning and coping normally, and that his or her personal safety is a concern.

Cognitive signs

- Slight disorientation becomes...   Can't tell own name, date, or describe event
- Problems prioritizing becomes...   Exclusive preoccupation
- Denial of severity becomes...   Denial of incident
- Flashbacks become...   Hallucinations
- Self-doubt becomes...   Paralysis
- Numbing becomes...   Disconnection
- Problems planning becomes...   Lifestyle dysfunction
- Confusion, misperceptions become...   Acting on bizarre beliefs

Emotional signs

- Upset, crying becomes...   Hysteria
- Anger, self-blame becomes...   Threat to others
- Dulled response becomes...   No response, rigidity
- Anxiety becomes...   Fetal position
- Fatigue, slowness becomes...   Physical shock or panic

Behavioral signs

- Excessive talking, laughter becomes...   Uncontrolled
- Restlessness, excitement becomes...   Unfocused agitation
- Frequent retelling becomes...   Ritualistic, continual acting
- Pacing, hand wringing becomes...   Ritualistic behavior
- Withdrawal becomes...   Immobility, rigidity
- Disheveled appearance becomes...   Can't care for self

Assessing factors that may increase vulnerability

Crisis affects everyone differently. There are certain factors that can increase individual vulnerability and affect how widespread and serious the effects of a traumatic event will be. Understanding the implications of these factors will help in dealing with the crisis and the individuals. According to Petersen and Straub (1992), Johnson (1993), and Sandoval (2013), the following factors may increase a student's vulnerability during a critical incident.

Critical event occurs within a closely-knit community

Often children come from neighborhoods where they have lived all their lives. A critical event occurring in the life of one student can affect most of the children that live in the community.

Critical event has multiple eyewitnesses

It is traumatic for any student to hear about the death of a peer. Witnessing the event has a much more serious effect.

Victim(s) had special significance

When the victim had special significance within the community many students tend to identify with them.

Community is exposed to widespread destruction or carnage

Widespread destruction, or several deaths in a community, will profoundly impact all members of the community.

Incident attracts a great deal of media attention

Often the media brings stories and events into the lives of students who may otherwise see the situation as being personally remote. The event may consequently seem more real to these students. More people may mourn the deceased.

Exposure to prior trauma

A recent or previous suicide, death, or other loss will make the individual more vulnerable to the negative effects of the current trauma.

Family crisis

Dysfunctional families may impair an individual's ability to cope effectively with a critical incident. Family structure and the responses taken by the family can result in successful resolution of a crisis for the individual at home or at school. Characteristics of a functional family are flexibility, affection, healthy adult relationships, healthy parent-child relationships, shared decision-making, common social activities, a healthy network of support with extended family members, and knowledge gained through previous crises and experiences. Dysfunctional families tend to be isolated within their own communities and do not exhibit the characteristics of a healthy family.

Pre-existing mental health issues

An individual with a mental illness will be more vulnerable to impairment of functioning. As well, individuals with a low developmental level, the inability to effectively regulate their own emotions, and the tendency to cope with crisis through avoidance are more vulnerable to psychological trauma.

Other characteristics

Feelings of inadequacy or physical fatigue will increase vulnerability to trauma.

ASSESSING FAMILY SUPPORT FOR CHILDREN

School crisis response teams do not normally provide direct support and services to families that are in a crisis state. It is possible that one of the crisis team members may deal with such a situation through the normal course of his or her work. It is helpful to determine the degree of available support for the affected individual, especially if the individual is having a great deal of difficulty coping with the crisis at school. This assessment is not meant to be an investigation into the family or to accumulate specific facts. It is possible that family support is impaired and that may be part of the problem. Thus, it is important to determine the family's contribution to the existing problem and ability to be part of the solution. When attempting to assess the level of family support consider the following points.

- Determine the composition of the current family and the basic interaction between members.

- Have there been past events within the family that could intensify coping with the current crisis?

- Determine the authority structure within the family, e.g. father, mother, grandparent, etc.

- Determine how decisions are made.

- Determine who tends to provide the most emotional support.

- Are there any divisions within the family that could affect decision-making?

- Has anyone in the family experienced a traumatic event that could affect his or her ability to assist the individual cope with the current crisis?

- Are there any current factors affecting the family's ability to cope? Consider illness, financial difficulties, recent move, marriage problems, etc.

Family impairment may be either moderate or serious. Moderate impairment within the family is indicated by its inability to meet the affected individual's emotional or physical needs. This would place additional stress on the family. Serious impairment within the family is indicated when the individual's basic needs cannot be met, or where there is potential for abuse or injury.

Recognizing the effects of trauma on children

Trauma can have both short-term and long-term effects on children (Johnson, 1989).

Short-term effects of trauma
- **frozen in place:** shock, disorientation, numbness
- **fight-or-flight response:** adrenaline pumps, heart races, hyperventilation occurs
- **exhaustion:** when fight-or flight can no longer be prolonged

- **shock:** disbelief, denial

- **cataclysm of emotions:** anger/rage, fear/terror, grief/sorrow, confusion/self-doubt

- reconstruction of emotional equilibrium

Long-term effects of trauma

- similar but milder reaction to trigger event

- grief due to losses

- flashbacks (often associated with guilt)

- recurrent dreams and fear of sleeping

- repetitive play with themes of trauma

- avoidance of reminders

- amnesia

- loss of recently acquired skills

- diminished interest

- numbed feelings

- sense of foreshortened future

- outbursts of anger

- concentration impairment

- hyperventilation

- reactions at time of anniversary of event

GRIEF AND THE GRIEF PROCESS

Dealing with grief is difficult work, both physically and emotionally. When an individual experiences a traumatic event where there is loss, that person will work through a grief process. When assisting grieving people, the goal is to take them beyond their initial reactions to the loss and get them to the point where they believe that they will survive. No two individuals work through the grief process at the same rate and their progression may not be linear. Remember this process takes time, effort, and determination.

The four goals or tasks of grief

Grief is a process. It is about sadness, tears, pain, anger, and loss. It is a healing process that allows us to eventually return to our normal state of daily functioning. Grief is also a process that requires active participation by the grieving individual. Things will not return to normal by attempting to wait for things to get better. Grieving children are faced with certain tasks

(Clayton 1994). The "Good Grief Program," developed by Sandra Fox, incorporates these four tasks:

- **Understand** – Grieving people must understand that death is universal. Everything that lives must die someday. This is not anybody's fault. They must understand that the deceased does not feel anything because his or her body does not function in the same way as when the person was alive. Finally, grieving people must understand that death is permanent, it is irreversible.

- **Grieve** – Grieving individuals must understand that there are many feelings associated with grieving. It is important for them to express and experience these feelings.

- **Commemorate** - Grieving individuals must remember the whole life of the deceased, and accept that the deceased had both good and bad characteristics.

- **Move on** - Once a grieving individual has moved through the grief process it is important for them to get on with his or her life.

The stages of grief and associated feelings

The stages of grief and the associated feelings in each stage are described below. Remember that individuals do not work through the stages of grief at the same rate and progression may not be linear.

Denial/shock

- feelings of numbness
- belief or feeling that deceased will return
- insomnia/sleeplessness
- loss of appetite (people literally forget to eat)
- inconsistent behavior
- bargaining with a deity
- persistent dreams or nightmares
- inability to concentrate
- preoccupation without being able to identify with what
- confusion

Fear

- nightmares
- sleeplessness
- easily startled
- anxiety and restlessness

53

- verbal expression of false bravado
- phobias

Guilt

- often masked by anger
- self-destructive behavior
- apologetic attitude
- acting out in response to praise or compliments

Depression (typical)

- lethargy
- decreased attention span
- frequent crying
- unkempt appearance
- disinterest in activities
- suicidal thoughts
- withdrawal from friends
- overeating or loss of appetite
- oversleeping or inability to sleep

Depression (masked)

- substance abuse
- consistent inappropriate joking
- involvement in high-risk behaviors
- gains reputation of "party person"
- sexual promiscuity
- adoption of an "I don't care" attitude

Reorganization

- Dreams of deceased become infrequent.
- Joy and laughter return.
- Planning for the future begins.
- Reinvestment in activities once dropped or forgotten.

Other emotional and physical signs of grief

Other emotional signs of grief may include feelings of sadness, guilt, anxiety, irritability, and loneliness.

Physical symptoms may include: uncontrollable bouts of crying; lack of concentration; indecision; loss of appetite; nausea, sensitivity to external stimuli such as noise, light and temperature; breathlessness; sleep disturbances; physical weakness; digestive upsets, and listlessness or lack of energy.

Note that individuals who react most strongly are those who were closest to the deceased. Also, individuals recovering from an earlier traumatic loss, emotional problems, or family difficulties may react strongly.

Signs of grief after a suicide

In the case of suicide, individuals who may have known about the suicide plan or been involved in a suicide pact are definitely at risk. Young children may associate the death with ghosts and spirits. Young children often think that the situation is reversible. They may develop a fear of being abandoned, worry about their parents' dying or be concerned about their own death. Some young children equate death with moving away, whereas others may see death as punishment for some wrongdoing.

Signs of grief specific to adolescents

Adolescents tend to move between adult and child-like behaviors. When a death has occurred, they may react with unexpected emotional intensity and confusion. To avoid the reality of death they may resort to excessive denial or withdrawal.

Recognizing age-specific reactions to loss

A child's age and perception of death must be taken into consideration when developing a crisis plan. There is a considerable difference between the way a child in first grade understands and perceives death and loss compared with an adolescent in eighth grade. For example, a child who is chronologically six years old but is at a developmental age of nine years, is emotionally six years old but is intellectually nine years old. Such a child can understand that death is final, but will still lack the coping skills to deal effectively with death. The following sections present age-specific reactions to death and loss, as reported by Petersen and Straub (1992):

Age 3-5

- often ask questions
- understand death as an ending
- believe that death is not permanent, person will return

- fear separation and abandonment

Age 5-10

- tend to express themselves mainly through music/art/play
- reduced attention span
- significant changes in behavior
- tend to fantasize about the event
- mistrust of adults
- tend to be very concrete in their understanding

Age 10-12 girls, 12-14 boys

- childlike in attitude
- anger at unfairness of the death
- excited about their survival
- may attribute symbolic meaning to the event
- tend to be self-judgmental
- may exhibit psychosomatic symptoms/illnesses

Age 13-18 girls, 15-18 boys

- tend to respond in adult-like manner
- tend to be judgmental
- morality crisis
- may move toward adult responsibilities to assume control
- tend to be suspicious and guarded
- may experience both sleeping and eating disorders
- may abuse both drugs and alcohol
- may tend to become impulsive

Things to expect when grieving

It is important to keep in mind that when there is a death or traumatic event there are certain things that you can expect about how you may respond to grief. You may find that:

- Your grief will take more energy than you believe it will.
- Your grief will take longer than most people think it should.

- Your grief will involve continual changes.

- Your grief will show itself in all spheres of your life: social, physical, emotional, thinking, and spiritual.

- Your grief will depend upon how you perceive the loss.

- You will grieve for many things (both symbolic and tangible), not just the death itself.

- You will grieve for what you have lost already, for the future, and for the hopes, dreams, and unfulfilled expectations you held for the deceased.

- Your grief will involve a wide variety of feelings and reactions: some expected, some not.

- You may have some identity confusion, due to the intensity and unfamiliarity of the grieving experience and uncertainty about your new role in the world.

- You may experience a combination of anger and depression, irritability, frustration, and intolerance.

- You may feel guilty in some form.

- You may have a lack of self-concern and poor self-worth.

- You may experience spasms, waves or acute upsurges of grief that occur without warning.

- You will have trouble thinking and making decisions, poor memory and organization.

- You may feel like you are going crazy.

- You may be obsessed with the death or preoccupied with thoughts of the dead person.

- You will search for meaning in/for your life and question your beliefs.

- You may respond inappropriately if others have unrealistic expectations about your mourning.

- You will have a few physical reactions.

- You will experience upsurges in your grief with certain dates, events, seasons and reminders.

- Certain experiences later in life may resurrect intense grief feelings for you (Rando, 1996).

What grieving individuals need

- outside help from relatives and friends

- someone who can help them process their most frightening thoughts and feelings (which may include attacking and blaming other family members)

- support of friends who attend a memorial service, and who drop by or stay in touch

- information about the grief process and resources they can use

- access to people who are comfortable talking about loss

- someone on whom they can displace their anger, pain, and frustration

PANIC ATTACKS

Panic attacks can be one response to adverse situations that induce fear. Panic attacks are characterized by "intense fear or intense discomfort that reach a peak within minutes, accompanied by physical and/or cognitive symptoms" (APA, 2013, p. 190). The individual may be able to know if a panic attack is oncoming or may experience an unexpected attack. Research has suggested that children ages 9-17 who experience panic attacks have a higher risk for psychopathologies, especially affective disorders (Goodwin and Gotlib, 2004). Over time certain situations may become associated with panic attacks (APA, 2013). Typically panic attacks start with the onset of intense apprehension, fear, or terror. Listed below are the major symptoms of a panic attack as listed in the Diagnostic and Statistical Manual of Mental Disorders, Fifth Edition (DSM-5) (APA, 2013).

Symptoms of panic attack

- palpitations, pounding heart, or accelerated heart rate

- sweating

- trembling or shaking

- sensations of shortness of breath or smothering

- feeling of choking

- chest pain or discomfort

- nausea or abdominal distress

- feeling dizzy, unsteady, light-headed, or faint

- chills or heat sensations

- paresthesia (numbness or tingling sensations)

- de-realization (feelings of unreality) or de-personalization (being detached from oneself)

- fear of losing control or "going crazy"

- fear of dying

POST-TRAUMATIC STRESS DISORDER (PTSD)

Post-traumatic stress disorder (PTSD) is a common human reaction that is a normal response to an abnormal event. PTSD can be devastatingly disruptive for years.

It is a trauma-related disorder that is, primarily, the result of experiencing traumatic event(s) (APA, 2013). PTSD symptoms can vary greatly across emotional, behavioral, and cognitive areas of function. A child with PTSD may exhibit symptoms that are not seen in another with PTSD because the range of symptoms is so great (Perry, 2002). The complexity of PTSD leads many children to be misdiagnosed with other disorders, such as separation anxiety or depression. Unless treated, PTSD can significantly affect the individual for the rest of his or her life (Flannery, 1999). It can lead to other disorders and medical conditions that may be co-morbid with or evolutions of PTSD. This disorder is a real concern for crisis intervention teams; all evidence of it should be treated seriously. Fortunately, PTSD can be prevented.

Reactions to trauma-inducing incidents occur in three phases:

(1) The **impact phase** occurs immediately following an event and can last minutes or days. During this phase, the person is either functioning mechanically (on "automatic") or is so stunned that he or she cannot act at all. Denial of the effects is common.

(2) The **recoil phase** can last a few days to several weeks. There is a great need to retell the story during this time. Individuals will also become overactive, particularly following any reminders of the event. The emotional reactions during this phase are angry outbursts, bouts of uncontrollable crying, and sometimes, panic attacks.

(3) The **post-traumatic stress disorder phase** begins weeks or even months after the event has occurred. People will feel a great sense of grief not only for whatever losses may have been sustained but also for the collapse of their assumptions and beliefs about the world. Survivor guilt is usually present, especially when a person benefits from the disaster. The destruction of assumptions (e.g., assumption of invulnerability, assumption that the world is meaningful, assumption of self-image) is often questioned during this period (Johnson, 1993).

The following two lists are simplified symptoms adapted from the DSM-5 diagnostic criteria for post-traumatic stress disorder (APA, 2013).

Symptoms of PTSD

- recurrent and intrusive recollections of the event
- nightmares
- dissociative reactions (e.g. flashbacks) that cause the individual to feel the event is recurring
- psychological and/or physiological distress experienced from exposure to perceived symbols and/or situations that resemble the traumatic event
- intentional avoidance of distressing memories, thoughts, reminders, or feelings related to the traumatic event
- problems recalling important details of traumatic event
- exaggerated negative beliefs of oneself and/or others

- distorted cognitions about cause and consequences of traumatic event (e.g. blaming)
- persistent negative emotional state
- loss of interest in activities
- feelings of detachment from others
- persistent inability to experience positive emotions

PTSD symptoms specific to children

- recurrent and intrusive recollections of the event
- nightmares
- dissociative reactions (e.g. flashbacks) that cause the individual to feel the event is recurring
- psychological and/or physiological distress experienced from exposure to perceived symbols and/or situations that resemble traumatic event
- intentional avoidance of distressing memories, thoughts, reminders, or feelings related to traumatic event
- substantially increased frequency of negative emotional states
- loss of interest in activities like play
- socially withdrawn behavior
- persistent reduction in expression of positive emotions
- irritable behavior and angry outbursts toward people or objects
- hyper-vigilance
- exaggerated startle response
- problems with concentration
- sleep disturbance

Post-trauma signs for elementary students

Cognitive signs
- confusion
- events
- sequencing
- inability to concentrate

Physical signs

- headaches
- complaints (headaches, stomach aches)
- itching
- sleep disturbances

Emotional signs

- fear of reoccurring, related event
- wanting to be fed, dressed
- school phobia, avoids groups
- responsibility, guilt over behavior
- aggression
- excessive concern re family safety

Behavioral signs

- clinging
- resumption of symptoms
- competition with siblings
- repetitive talking, re-enacting events
- disobedience
- drop in school performance
- nightmares

Post-trauma signs for junior/senior high students

Cognitive signs

- problems concentrating
- excessive concern about health

Physical signs

- headaches
- vague complaints, pain
- skin rashes

- loss of appetite, overeating

Emotional signs

- depression
- anxiety

Behavioral signs

- fails to meet responsibilities
- resumes earlier coping styles
- withdraws socially
- exhibits antisocial behavior
- experiences survivor guilt
- abuses drugs or alcohol
- decline in school performance
- suddenly shifts in attitude, styles
- acts "too old, too soon"
- drops out, pregnancy, marriage
- makes precipitous life decisions
- sudden changes in relationships

Preventing PTSD

There are several strategies used to reduce and/or eliminate post-traumatic stress disorder in children, adolescents, and adults (Johnson, 1993). The most frequently used strategies include defusing emotions, group discussions and debriefings (individual and group). These procedures should be offered to both staff and students.

Defusing emotions

Following any violent crisis, the school counselor(s) or crisis response team member should ensure that all students directly affected are given an opportunity to "defuse" their emotions before they go home, and to attend debriefing over the next three days. The goal of defusing is to lessen tension or restore calm. Students should also receive ongoing counseling if needed. They should have access to legal assistance, if required, and protection from reminders of the incident.

Attendance at both defusing and debriefing sessions should be mandatory for all students directly affected. The students and staff exposed to the tragic incident must talk with each other prior to leaving that day. Do not defuse students who were directly affected by or witnessed the incident with any other students. If this happens you run the risk of increasing the emotionality in the less affected students.

Defusing emotions involves ventilation of thoughts and emotions immediately following a traumatic event. It is the first step in starting to deal with the critical incident. Defusing is an unstructured activity that is conducted by the counselor, school psychologist, or other school-based crisis team member who is familiar with the process.

The procedure for defusing emotions is presented below.

Procedure for defusing emotions

Adapted from Johnson (1993)

(1) Provide information and include parents if they come to school.

(2) Keep everyone together for some time (groups of 15-20).

(3) Promote ventilation by asking:

   o What was the worst part for you?

   o Where were you when it happened? (Listen!)

(4) Prepare students and parents for reactions of:

   o sleeplessness

   o lack of concentration

   o nausea

   o crying

   o irritability

   o demanding

   o fear and anxiety

   o nightmares

   o sweating

   o numbness

   o withdrawal

   o clinging

(5) Let them know that these reactions are normal.

(6) Give them suggestions for coping.

(7) Let them know when follow-up will be provided.

Debriefing

Following the defusing, individual and classroom debriefings are conducted. Debriefings begin the process of putting the incident and people's reactions to the incident into perspective. They may be conducted either individually or in a group. Usually debriefings are implemented during the first day, or, if the traumatic event occurred on a weekend, the first day after the weekend. Debriefing for staff is usually scheduled for the following day after school. Debriefings include several phases which, once started, cannot be interrupted, even if they must go beyond class time.

The procedures for conducting debriefing are covered in detail in Step 6: Review the situation and "debrief."

SOLUTION-FOCUSED BRIEF THERAPY (SFBT)

Solution-focused brief therapy (SFBT) is a strengths-based model of therapy that builds from the client's successes, where he or she wants to go from the current situation, and how he or she wants to get there (Trepper et al., n.d.). SFBT is conversational in nature with the therapist becoming fully invested in the solution by helping the client construct it (Trepper et al., n.d.) Research on the effectiveness of SFBT is small compared to major therapeutic models. Most SFBT studies indicate that it yields positive results (Woods et al., 2011).

The use of solution-focused brief therapy offers a practical, time-sensitive intervention for a variety of school problems. More importantly SFBT is a positive approach to dealing with difficulties or issues that may be hard for students to overcome on their own.

In the context of crisis intervention, this therapy is an approach that, although short-term, is targeted at those individuals who are having difficulty overcoming their grief and loss, as manifest through panic attacks or post-traumatic stress disorder. In a school setting, its implementation may be within the realm of school counselors who have been professionally trained to engage in counseling. Those who are not qualified to offer counseling should not attempt to use SFBT (as outlined below). This description is offered for information only. It will increase understanding of the positive impact that counselors can have in schools when providing post-crisis support to students.

The use of SFBT assumes the following:

- All individuals have resources and are already doing something to try and solve their problems.

- The goal of SFBT is to identify and use these resources in the student's best interest.

- Change is constant, sometimes the problem will be present other times it will not.

- Individuals are more likely to change if they define the goals and generate solutions that work for them.

- At times change can occur quickly.

- Sometimes all that is needed is a small change to prompt other changes in the individual's life.

The use of SFBT requires that the counselor be familiar with the necessary key skills and strategies listed below.

- use of solution-focused language

- use of solution-focused questions, which help construct exceptions and potential solutions

- use of future questions to present a picture of life after the problem has been solved

- use of scaling questions to help define realistic goals

- use of direct and indirect compliments

- ability to assign "doing" or "observation" tasks, dependent upon the individual's readiness to change

SFBT procedure for solution-focused counseling

A guide to implementing SFBT is included below. You will note that at the top of the outline, three types of clients are listed: visitor, complainant, and customer. Visitors tend to be more resistive to change whereas customers are actively seeking solutions to their problems. Complainants are only interested in complaining about things, not seeking solutions.

☐ Visitor

☐ Complainant

☐ Customer

(1) Establish rapport.

o Exchange greetings.

(2) Determine the purpose.

o How can I help?

o What brings you here?

(3) Define the problem.

o What problem you would like to solve?

o How will you know this meeting has been successful?

(4) Discuss ideas about goal setting.

o When the problem is solved what will be different?

o Use miracle questions.

o Suppose that the problem is solved.

(5) Explore exceptions.

o When were things a little better?

o Explore exceptions to the problem.

o Explore previous solutions.

o Explore pre-treatment changes.

o Explore the ending of the problem sequence.

- o Explore potential solution patterns.
- o Amplify miracle questions.
- o Explore coping questions.

(6) Normalize and validate the situation.
- o It's been tough.

(7) Take a "think break."
- o Write down what impressed you about the individual.
- o Use the client's key phrases and words.
- o Put together suggestions to share with the client.

(8) Share ideas.
- o Summarize what impresses you.
- o Validate the client's struggle to solve the problem.
- o Suggest strategies to try.

(9) Determine and assign actions/tasks for the client.
- o If it works, do more of it.
- o If it is not working, do something different.
- o Amplify exceptions.
- o Use observation tasks.
- o Do something different.
- o Pretend.
- o Try a coin toss.
- o Create a surprise task.

(10) Ask scaling questions.
- o What is the client's investment in change?
- o What is the client's confidence in change?
- o Progress to date?
- o Goal setting?
- o What needs to happen to move you up one notch?

(11) Set goals.
- o Choose small goals.
- o Make them specific and concrete.
- o Make them realistic and achievable.
- o Presence of something.

- o Build on solution pattern.
- o Perceived as hard work.

(12) Use the client's language.

- o Use client's language.
- o State the problem in past tense.
- o Open possibilities through re-framing.

WHAT TO DO

Step 6: Review the situation and "debrief"

DEBRIEFING

You may have heard the term "debrief" or "debriefing." There are many situations in life where it is helpful to review what has happened, ask questions about what went right and what went wrong, and discuss what was learned from it. Following a crisis, counselors and psychologists will undertake a "debrief," or a systematic review of the events which led to the event, what happened during the crisis and afterwards. The debriefing may focus on an individual student or a classroom. In some situations, school crisis team members or teachers can undertake a debriefing.

Classroom debriefing

The debriefing model discussed in this section is adapted from Critical Incident Stress Debriefing (CISD), a process-oriented supportive intervention program (Mitchell, n. d.) This model is group-oriented and designed for "group cohesion and unit performance" (Mitchell, n.d., pp. 2). This model is not to take the place of psychotherapy and is meant to supplement additional crisis intervention programs and techniques.

If a critical incident affects a substantial number of individuals, it is preferable to conduct classroom debriefings (critical incident stress debriefings). There are several **exceptions** to this guideline:

- The individual student shows signs of being seriously impaired due to the crisis.

- The class is not supportive of one another.

- The students' needs vary widely.

- The class is highly polarized on the issues.

- Involved families are highly affected by the event.

- Students who were directly affected by, or witnessed the incident should not be debriefed with any other students. To do so you run the risk of increasing the emotionality in the less affected students. For these students, debriefing should be done privately. Adolescents tend to "feed" off the emotions of each other.

Classroom debriefings are simply structured group discussions, not psychotherapy. They allow the class, as a group, to sort out the facts leading to the incident and express their reactions to it. The classroom debriefing provides a format that enables the crisis team member to put the incident and individuals' reactions in perspective, as well as clarifying any misinformation. Debriefings also attempt to salvage group cohesiveness from the disintegrating effects of a crisis. Classroom debriefings are usually implemented on the same day as the incident or a day later. Classroom debriefings can be conducted with all grades except kindergarten and some first grade classes (evaluate classroom using exceptions listed above). At the lower elementary school level, they tend to be shorter in length and are not as emotional as the junior/senior grades' debriefings may be. Helpers are reminded not to present graphic details about how a victim died. Likewise, if a child asks for specific details state only how the individual died and then move on to another question.

A useful strategy when conducting classroom debriefings is to assign a staff member (e.g., the classroom teacher) to assist the school crisis team member. A staff member can provide the necessary background information about students in the class who may be experiencing other traumatic events or outcomes from a dysfunctional family. This staff member can also be of considerable help in identifying those students at risk. When the principal has requested support from the district/division, or a crisis team member has been dispatched to the school for political purposes or due to policy/procedures, that individual may assist the school crisis member when conducting debriefings.

A few basic ground rules when conducting a classroom debriefing are provided below.

(1) Have all students form a large circle, either seated at the desks or on the floor.

(2) Have an object, such as a feather, stick, special rock, or some other object, that can be used to identify the current speaker.

(3) Have a box of tissues readily at hand.

(4) Do not have family members present in the class.

(5) Clearly state the ground rules.

Classroom debriefing model

Adapted from Mitchell and Everly (1993)

(1) **Introductory phase** - The leader lays down the basic rules for participation.

    o   Leader presents introduction and purpose.

    o   Confidentiality is paramount (what's said in here stays in here); no notes, taping, recording.

    o   No interrupting.

    o   No put-downs.

    o   No blaming of anyone.

- o Speak only for yourself.
- o Pass if you do not want to speak.
- o Everyone is equal.

(2) **Fact phase** - Here students explore and gain concurrence on the sequence of events, and role each played in the incident.

- o What happened?
- o Who was involved?
- o When did it happen?
- o Where did it happen?
- o How did it happen?

(3) **Thought phase**

- o What was the first thing you thought about?

(4) **Reaction phase**

- o What was the worst thing about incident?
- o What was your first reaction?
- o How are you reacting now?
- o What effect has this had on you?

(5) **Symptom phase**

- o Each student is given the opportunity to share.
- o What unusual things did you experience at the time?
- o What unusual things are you experiencing now?
- o Has your life changed in any way at home and school?

(6) **Teaching phase** - The leader provides information to the students regarding normal reactions to the incident, and anticipates later reactions. Any misconceptions regarding the incident or its effects can be cleared up.

- o You are 100% normal if you have any of these feelings, thoughts, and symptoms: Denial, avoidance, sleep difficulties, irritability, fatigue, restlessness, depression/mood swings, difficulty concentrating, nightmares, vomiting/diarrhea, suspiciousness.
- o How have you coped with difficulties before?
- o What are you doing to cope now?
- o How will you know that things are getting better for you?

(7) **Closure phase**

- o Remind students of strengths.

o   Reassure them that it will take time to heal.

o   Reassure them that you will be there.

o   Any other questions?

o   Want to add something?

Individual debriefing

Individual debriefing is a more effective method for dealing with students who were close to the victim or are having difficulty putting the critical incident into perspective. Following any crisis, the school counselor(s) or crisis team member should ensure that all students directly affected attend a debriefing session over the next two days. Students should also receive ongoing counseling if needed. Attendance at debriefing sessions should be mandatory for all students directly affected. Information in the procedure below has been adapted from Johnson (1993).

Individual debriefing procedure

Adapted from Johnson (1993)

(1) **Find privacy** - Attempt to find a comfortable, private place for the conference. If the conference is to be individual, it must be private to engage trust. Avoid placing yourself in what may be perceived as a compromising position, particularly if you are male, and with a female student. Stay visible to others.

(2) **Maintain calm** - Probably, the student is experiencing uncertainty and self-doubt. Presenting a balanced demeanor tells the student that what he or she is about to say will be accepted.

(3) **Be honest with yourself** - Keep in touch with your own feelings and reactions to the student, the issues, and the situation. If you feel you cannot handle the situation, ask someone else to take over, and arrange a transition.

(4) **Read between the lines** - Watch the student's behavior. Be aware of subtle messages. Draw inferences for further exploration.

(5) **Validate feelings** - Feelings are neither right nor wrong. Whatever the feelings the student is experiencing, validate them. Often feelings clamor for expression; help the student clarify them.

(6) **Listen well** - Good listening involves several skills. Use gentle probes for clarification and elaboration. Maintain good eye contact. Use increasingly focused questions when appropriate (especially when you suspect the individual capable of self-destructive behavior). Trust your hunches and check them out.

(7) **Show belief** - Your job at this point is to listen and to facilitate expression. You are not a judge, jury, or investigator. Show confidence, trust, and faith that what the students is saying is the truth as he or she believes it to be.

(8) **Dispel fault** - If the student was victimized, be sure to explain that the incident

was not his or her fault. Be proactive about this, because victims tend to distrust themselves and others, and blame themselves. Assure them that they were not responsible for the incident. If the incident is due to a suicide, dispel any feelings that they could have prevented it.

(9) **Explore fears** - Individuals can often tell about what happened to them, but may be unable to express assumptions they have made, questions they have, or fears they may hold about the incident. Facilitating the expression of these assumptions, questions, and fears at this point empowers the individuals to deal with them.

(10) **Provide information** - The right information at the right time can be very helpful. If you know something about the incident, normal reactions to that type of incident, or actions that could be taken, consider sharing it, Be sure not to preach and be careful that your own need to "do something" is not clouding your judgment regarding the timeliness of the information.

(11) **Walk through the process** - Many processes are predictable, given a situation. Loss of a significant person will predictably involve the grief process. Disclosure of crime or victimization will predictably involve the police and legal procedures. When the time is right, share what you know about certain procedures that can assist the student in predicting and planning for his or her near future.

(12) **Explore resources** - As soon as possible, explore with the student what resources are available, and what his or her support system provides. Assist the student in deciding to whom, when, and how to "reach out" for that support.

Group debriefing

Following a critical incident, students need a chance to talk about it. They do not, however, need to be coerced. Group debriefing is a useful format for students to state their feelings about the incident in a less formal setting. Make sure every student is asked questions at each step of the process, but also set a rule that at any time anyone can say "pass" and not answer. Group debriefing sessions tend to be somewhat more structured than defusing sessions. Group debriefing is usually implemented the second or third day after the incident and can signify some movement towards resolution.

Group debriefing procedure

(1) **State the ground rules** - Ground rules can vary from group to group, but some will remain the same. Here are a few of the standard ground rules to follow:

o   Confidentiality is paramount (what's said in here stays in here).

o   No put-downs.

o   No interrupting.

o   Speak only for yourself.

(2) **Decide on a format** - A good way to handle discussing facts and feelings is to first go around the room asking individuals what they saw and when they became aware

of the incident. Later go around asking what individuals heard. Finally, ask what they felt. This pattern establishes the principle of sharing, while it moves from cognitive to affective material.

(3) **Discuss needs -** Students may need to talk about similar incidents both current and past. This is all part of the sorting out process, and may occupy much of the time allotted.

(4) **Gauge reactions -** Student's emotional reactions can vary widely. They can range from unaffected or amused, to being quite shaken. An unaffected reaction, however, may be numbness. General amusement is often a defense against anxiety. Such students may need to be protected from others seeking to displace anger.

(5) **When it's over -** Keep the discussion gently focused until it has gone its normal routine. Expect students to refer to the event and to return to discussing it in the future.

(6) **Assess the need for further support -** Evaluate whether students need further support (that is, if individuals are uncontrollable or seem to be in shock), and refer to the office or to whatever back up is available right away.

Interactions to avoid during debriefing

- **False promises -** Don't say things you are not sure of, or are not true. If you are unsure of something, tell them "I'm not sure, but I will find out for you." Do not say, "Everything is going to be all right!" unless you have some way of knowing that for certain.

- **Falling apart -** It's all right to shed some tears in empathy with another person, but it is essential to remain in emotional control. Don't fall apart or react with excessive emotion, because that sends the message that you can't be trusted with the information. The student has enough to cope with; he or she does not need to be forced to take care of your emotional problems as well.

- **Casting judgments -** Facial expression, body language, inferences, and questions can each communicate judgments. Even, "Why did you take so long to come to me?" signals an implied judgment, which can be more than a traumatized student can handle. Focus on the person, not upon what's right.

- **Inquisition -** Don't play detective, searching for information to hang the perpetrator. Such inquisition will only drive the student away or make things worse. Instead, assist the student in revealing what he or she feels is necessary.

- **Clichés, euphemisms, and overly general comments -** Avoid using such phrases and comments as "gone to sleep," "if you need anything," or "I know you must have so many feelings now." These general statements suggest insincerity.

FACTORS THAT CAN AFFECT THE ABILITY TO RESPOND EFFECTIVELY

There are factors that can potentially affect the ability of a crisis team member to respond effectively to individuals and a critical incident (Petersen and Straub, 1992).

Common factors

- prior suicide in family
- unresolved feelings of grief
- marital or relationship problems
- financial difficulties
- personal health problems
- fatigue
- loss of, or lack of, positive feelings towards victim
- isolation and withdrawal
- a history of, and current, personal anxiety
- rigidity in thinking and resistance to change
- suspicion and paranoia
- fear that it will not get better
- fear of losing control

Associated factors

- **Fear about liability** - Many professionals facing crisis intervention situations suddenly become aware of their professional vulnerability. Specific fears over professional responsibilities and legal liabilities are legitimately raised.

- **Guilt** - Commonly, professionals feel guilt at not seeing the signs of a crisis sooner, or of not acting sooner than they did. Of all professional groups, teachers seem to be the most prone to guilt.

- **Inadequacies** - When confronted with catastrophic situations, staff members often feel that they can do little to "fix the pain." The expectation that "I should be able to fix it" leads to feelings of helplessness.

- **Anger** - Feelings of anger and rage are often the result of dealing with children who have been victimized by adults.

- **Desire to protect** - Listening to painful and unfortunate situations often creates a desire to provide 100% protection for the child, 100% of the time. Obviously, this is impossible, and usually the damage has already occurred. This creates further frustration.

- **Distrust** - Distrust of the home situation, the law enforcement system, and the crisis intervention team is natural. The distrust is fueled by the "what-ifs." What if the perpetrator gets out? What if the police can't catch him or her? What if he or she gets a light sentence? What if the parents take it out on the child? What if?

- **Old personal issues** – Sometimes a student's critical incident or life situation parallels your own past or present. While this can create shared experience, rapport, and understanding, it can also create discomfort, pain, and significant distraction. The adult's unfinished business can interfere with his or her ability to focus on the student and can drain needed energy.

- **Post-crisis vulnerability** - Extensive involvement, unfinished business, or the intensity of the situation can leave you in great emotional turmoil. A sense of emptiness and self-doubt later may prevail. Find a support person who can help.

STRESS AND SELF CARE

Self care is important to the mental and physical health of anyone who is undergoing stressful periods of work. Richards et al. loosely defined self care to their research participants as "any activity that one does to feel good about oneself. It can be categorized into four groups which include: physical, psychological, spiritual, and support" (2010, p. 252). They found that overall well-being is associated with taking the time to take of one's self by participating in self-care activities (as perceived by the individual) and making self-care a priority. It is extremely important and ethically imperative for those who work in areas such as crisis intervention to consciously make time for self-care for the benefit of themselves and their clients.

Handling a crisis that involves students is draining and difficult. During a crisis, routines are disrupted, different management skills are called for, and emotions are subjected to a roller-coaster ride. The level of stress is compounded by the fact that student crises are rarely "fixable." Usually, there are no clear resolutions and there are no clear criteria of what is or is not successful intervention. Only with experience can professionals walk away from an intervention feeling, "Yes, that worked well," or "No, that really did not work out." There are no standards, no norms, and no evaluation system to tell us how we have done.

Stress works in an interactive cycle, with reaction to stressful situations compounding the situation itself, creating more stress. Stress management involves long-range planning, focusing upon our expectations, our manner of interpreting situations, and evaluating the way our behaviors make situations worse.

In the short term, it is useful to have several brief stress-breaking techniques available to use for yourself. A useful strategy is to plan time slots of five to ten minutes during the day when you can be by yourself. Use a relaxation technique prior to going home, such as brief meditation, self-hypnosis, or listening to a stress reduction tape. Share your reaction to the incident with someone else.

Everyone manifests stress differently, but there are four general areas of impact: physical, psychological, family, and work. The type of impact can provide clues for working out an effective stress management plan. To reduce the effects of post-traumatic stress in staff, it is important to take care of your own needs before, during, and after the critical incident has passed (Johnson, 1993).

Important aspects of self care before a critical incident

- Increase your knowledge and skills.
- Become aware of your own "hot spots" and personal triggers.
- Become aware of your needs and the amount of stress you can handle.
- Accumulate background information about stress and self care.

Self care during a critical incident

- Don't ignore your own feelings and personal needs.
- Set limits for yourself.
- Don't drink excessive amounts of caffeine and/or alcohol.
- Remain constantly aware of your feelings.
- Exercise vigorously within twenty-four hours, if medically approved. This will burn off any excess chemicals in the body caused by stress.
- Retain a safe distance from issues.
- Eat balanced meals and get plenty of sleep.
- Talk about the incident with your spouse, friends, and colleagues.
- Seek out help when you are in need.
- Set specific alone time for yourself and stick to it.

Self care after a critical incident

- Reflect upon the incident and your reactions by yourself and with support persons.
- Debrief with colleagues when necessary.
- Talk about your feelings and reactions to the incident at home.

THE NEED FOR MULTICULTURAL AWARENESS

When responding to a critical incident, you may be faced with children who are part of a different culture. To work effectively with these children, consider the following points.

- Get to know as much as possible about the culture.
- Be aware of your own cultural biases and beliefs.

- Always seek clarification if you do not understand what an individual has said.

- Don't assume that you know or understand what an individual's nonverbal communication means unless you are familiar with his or her culture.

- Be aware of any of your own non-verbal communication that may be perceived as insulting in other cultures.

- Don't impose your personal values.

- Remain objective.

- Do not judge others from different cultures by your own cultural values.

- Remember that your lack of familiarity with a specific culture may increase the stress during the intervention.

- Remember that you cannot change a person's cultural perspective.

- Continually attempt to increase your awareness of your personal preconceptions and stereotypes of the cultures with which you may be working.

Native American traditions – healing circles

Healing circles are an element of Native American spirituality. A healing circle can be a useful response to a critical incident.

During a healing circle a feather, stick, or some other object used to identify the current speaker is passed around the circle. Only the person holding the object is permitted to speak. Interruptions are not allowed when the individual holding the object is speaking, as it is considered rude and inappropriate. Once the circle has been formed, outsiders should not attempt to arbitrarily jump in without being accepted or welcomed into the group. Wait to be invited into the group. This procedure is easy to implement and has been used by some Native Americans for hundreds of years. Using a healing circle works well when conducting a classroom debriefing.

Healing circle procedure

(1) Ask students to form a circle, seated either on chairs or the floor.

(2) Introduce the procedure. The format is like the classroom debriefing.

(3) Once the group has moved through the introduction and fact phases, give the "talking feather," stone, or stick to one individual to start the process. If the individual does not wish to speak, the object is passed to the person next to him or her.

   o Remember that interruptions are strictly prohibited. It is most important not to interrupt the individual who has possession of the talking stone or feather.

   o Once a healing circle has been formed, outsiders should not attempt to join the circle unless invited.

   o When a healing circle is used, it is most important to respect the process and those individuals involved in it.

WHAT TO DO

Step 7: Organize a memorial service – involve students

DETERMINING AN APPROPRIATE RESPONSE

If a traumatic event involving a death has occurred in your school, the principal must decide the appropriate response by the school.

It is important that there be a helpful and appropriate response when there is a death in the school, whether it is due to accident, natural causes, or suicide. Often in small communities the school is the focal point of attention. The school not only functions as an educational facility for the children, but as a recreational center for the community.

Consider how the individual(s) died

How the individual or individuals died will, in part, determine the type of response by the school. If an individual died because of suicide, the response should be "low key." An elaborate or high profile response may draw unwanted attention to the way in which the individual died. When suicide is the cause of death, there is the fear of copycat deaths or pacts between close friends of the deceased. Any attempts to glorify the way in which the individual died should be discouraged. Glorification of suicide may inadvertently be accomplished by holding a large memorial service at the school, students establishing a shrine at the deceased student's desk or locker, or by drawing undo attention to the way the individual died. Regardless, most students will want to hold some form of memorial service for the deceased.

ORGANIZING A SCHOOL MEMORIAL SERVICE

Purpose

Remember that a school memorial service is not a substitute for an actual funeral service. The school service is a time for accepting and grieving the loss of one of its members. It is an opportunity to say goodbye.

Timing

The service should be short. Hold the service at a time that is least likely to cause disruption in the school routine. A good time to schedule the school service is either at the beginning or end of the day, especially at the start of a weekend (Friday afternoon). This provides a natural break from school. Students will be at home for two days or more where they can receive support and comfort from parents rather than being continually exposed to and "feeding" off the emotionality of others.

Discussing and coordinating with the family of the deceased

It is most important to discuss the proposed school memorial service with the family of the deceased and invite them to the service. Encourage peers and family members to participate in the service. Be aware of the deceased person's religion and, if appropriate, discuss the service with the deceased person's priest, minister, rabbi, imam, or religious leader. Make separate arrangements for those who do want to attend the service. Before holding the service, it is important to determine the potential numbers of people attending so that proper accommodations can be arranged. If the weather permits, the service may be held outdoors.

Record keeping

Complete the **Memorial service record** to organize a memorial service at the school and to help keep track of the process.

PREPARING STUDENTS FOR THE MEMORIAL SERVICE

It is important for teachers to prepare their students for what to expect at a memorial service. Many young people have never been to a funeral service. Discussing the memorial and will help reduce the anxiety and fear. Students should know what to expect and what to say during the service. Knowing what to say and do during a memorial of a student with a different ethnic or religious background from their own may be particularly important.

It is important to involve those students closest to the deceased individual in the planning of activities and the actual memorial service. This will help bring a sense of closure to the critical incident. An effective way to resolve grief is to actively participate in the commemoration of a death. In addition, many students will want to send messages (perhaps cards and letters) to the grieving family. Others will want to create a tribute from the class.

After the memorial, it is important to gather the students and take them back to their classrooms to give them an opportunity to discuss their feelings and reactions. Time is needed for comfort and direction. This time will help students bring closure to the incident.

CLASSROOM ACTIVITIES TO HELP BRING CLOSURE

Listed below are constructive, participatory classroom activities that facilitate the resolution of a critical incident. These activities involve one or more students. It is important that any activity be in good taste and not go against the known wishes and beliefs of the family. Participation in an activity is a positive way in which to remember the deceased and to help bring closure to the incident (Greenstone and Leviton, 1993).

- Have the class write a poem.

- Write a letter, or make a special card or other item for the parents.

- Draw a picture of the student.

- Send flowers to the family.

- Send a basket of fruit to the family.

- Write a song about the deceased.

- Plant a tree.

- Attend the funeral service.

- Name a trophy after the person.

- Set up a bulletin board in the person's memory.

- Make a garden.

- Collect donations for the family.

- Place a dedication in the yearbook.

- Display a special picture, painting, or sculpture as a memorial to the student.

WHAT TO DO

Step 8: Deal with crisis aftermath

BE AWARE THAT STAFF MAY BE TRAUMATIZED

Crisis team members are at risk for vicarious traumatization and burnout simply because they may work with individuals who are traumatized (whether identified or not). These are results of trauma work and may be compounded by the fact that crisis team members will more than likely know the affected individuals of a crisis on a personal level leaving them to be psychologically or physically compromised (Nickerson et al., 2006). It is important for all those on teams working with traumatized individuals, including administration, to be educated about vicarious traumatization (Trippany et al., 2004) as well as burnout and compassion fatigue.

Vicarious traumatization

Vicarious traumatization is defined by Pearlman and Mac Ian (1995) "as the transformation that occurs within the therapist (or other trauma worker) because of empathic engagement with clients' trauma experiences and their sequelae." (p. 558) Vicarious traumatization affects the individual both introspectively and introspectively (Pearlman and Mac Ian, 1995).

Helpers working with traumatized individuals are, to some degree, likely to become traumatized as well. Conducting individual and classroom debriefings, as well as being continually exposed to the emotional responses of people reacting to a critical incident is difficult and painful.

Vicarious trauma may not warrant clinical intervention, but it can make life miserable until the incident passes. The most obvious risk to individuals who work with grief-stricken, depressed, or suicidal individuals is that they can end up exhibiting many of the same symptoms (Johnson 1993).

Signs of vicarious trauma

- anxious
- depressed
- distrustful
- irritable
- ineffective

- suspicious

- pessimistic

- alienated

Burnout

Burnout is a state in which people find themselves feeling that their work is hopeless, that they are not capable of doing their work, or that they cannot emotionally cope with their work (Stamm, 2005). Burnout is characterized by three main dimensions: "overwhelming exhaustion, feelings of cynicism and detachment from the job, and a sense of ineffectiveness and lack of accomplishment" (Maslach et al., 2001, p. 399).

Acute stress response (ASR) and depression

Some staff members may develop an acute stress response (ASR) to the critical incident. Symptoms of ASR are feeling overworked, frequent crying, withdrawal, lack of interest in social events, and reduced exercise. Some staff members may remain unusually quiet. These individuals may be experiencing signs of depression.

HELP TRAUMATIZED STAFF

According to Pross, self-care, self-examination, focused supervision, and therapy training are all effective ways of preventing both burnout and vicarious traumatization (2006). Crisis team workers need to know their personal limits and recognize when they are showing signs of vicarious traumatization and/or burnout.

For some individuals, all that may be needed is rest, refreshment, and possibly a rotation to a less critical assignment. Those who have a more serious reaction to the incident may need to be placed on a light duty assignment or be allowed to return home for a period of recovery.

Any staff member who shows signs of acute stress response should be referred for counseling with trained personnel (Johnson, 1993). This may result in a referral to an employee assistance program (EAP) counselor. Information about an EAP program should be made available to all staff.

Expect reactions and provide understanding

It is wise for the principal to schedule a debriefing for all staff members. The procedure to follow for debriefing staff is like the format used for classroom debriefings.

Remember that when talking with traumatized staff, the individual may be in shock or feeling vulnerable. When individuals are in this state, they need an understanding authority figure who can convince them that things are under control. If they need to cry allow them to do so.

It is important for the principal to expect and tolerate staff reactions to the incident, so long as those reactions do not interfere with the students and the rest of the staff. After the incident, staff members should not be told what or how to feel. Remember that feelings are neither right nor wrong but they are real. This is also a time to avoid a critique of staff performance, other than to acknowledge a job well done.

The following points will help to reduce some of the accumulated stress that staff experience during a critical incident.

- Share information about expected reactions, and alert staff to the potential for delayed responses to the incident.

- Explore support systems and suggest sources for additional help. This helps the individual utilize existing support and provides direction.

- Let staff members know you will continue to be available to them.

Be aware of "hot spots"

Past events like the current incident tend to remind us of our own weaknesses and issues that we may have been trying to avoid. These hot spots may cause us to focus on one issue and not on others. Consequently, we may make bad judgments and ignore other pressing issues. Such hot spots will also increase our stress and vulnerability to trauma.

Often we are not aware of our own hot spots. When we are aware of our hot spots we are in a better position to remove ourselves from the situation. When we are not aware, we will become alerted to our vulnerability by our emotional and physical reactions.

It is important for team members to be aware of their own reactions because those reactions can indicate other unresolved issues and conflicts or difficulty dealing with the current incident.

The following list indicates feelings that may be experienced by a crisis team member as well as some possible implications of those feelings.

Feelings:	Possible implications of those feelings:
Anxiousness	Avoiding something, fatigue
Distraction	Picking up on nonverbal message
Coldness	Over-identification with incident
Physical discomfort	Unfinished personal business
Sense of being overwhelmed	Manipulation of individuals

Monitor psychological distancing by team members

Crisis team members should understand that it is impossible for them to attempt to remain unmoved by the incident. They remain less affected if they can psychologically distance themselves from the incident and engage in self-care in the evenings.

Psychological distancing refers to the level of individual receptivity or way the helper responds to an individual needing support. This degree of receptivity can indicate how effective or ineffective the helper may be. Listed below are the different levels of receptivity, as identified by Johnson (1993):

- absent
- confused
- identifies
- distant
- sympathetic
- objective
- empathetic

The two most destructive psychological characteristics that a crisis responder may exhibit are absence and confusion. If the responder is psychologically absent, the victim learns that he or she is not worth the energy or effort it takes the responder to listen. If the responder is confused, it confuses and disorients the victim.

A crisis team member who is distant may not provide the victim with the necessary validation and support. If team members over-identify they may not provide the victim a balanced perspective.

To be most effective, a crisis team member should be objective, empathetic, and sympathetic. Crisis response members must develop a sense of their own receptivity and what is comfortable for them.

GAINING PERSPECTIVE AFTER THE INCIDENT

The time to help students and staff put a crisis in perspective occurs when the incident is over and emotional and physical exhaustion have set in. At this point, there will be time for the affected individuals to:

- Search for meaning in the event.
- Understand and accept their emotional reactions.
- Increase their ability to cope with future adversities.

During this time, you can also do the following:

- Promote maturity and growth in the students and staff.
- Integrate the emotional investment of the students into a loyalty towards their school.
- Refine and/or revise your crisis response plan.

Debriefing school staff

In the aftermath of a crisis, you must debrief school staff. It is important to include all support personnel, including secretaries and custodians. The principal should schedule time for staff members to attend a debriefing within the first three days of the incident, usually on the second or third day. The debriefing can be co-facilitated by both the counselor/school psychologist and the principal. Attendance at the debriefing should be strongly encouraged.

The procedure used to debrief school staff is the classroom debriefing model presented in Step 6: Review the situation and "debrief." Teachers should be asked about their reactions to the events of the day and for their input for improvement. The discussion should end with ideas for self care, with participants encouraged to commit to doing one nice thing for themselves (going for a back massage, buying a special treat, going out for a nice meal at a favorite restaurant, etc.).

Debriefing school/district/division crisis teams

In the aftermath of a crisis, school based and district/division crisis teams must be debriefed. Debriefing at this level tends to follow an operational debriefing format. This format is followed because both teams are concerned with improving their overall performance.

It is important to note that there may be a difference of opinion between school team members and district/division crisis members as to how the school responded. There may be questions about the level of district/division support, and about who should have overseen the school crisis team, and what actions should have taken place. School team members may be in an emotionally fragile state. Criticism and condemnation from district/department personnel can have a particularly destructive effect on the school crisis team. It is best if school and department crisis teams conduct independent debriefings.

The operational debriefing format described below is suggested for both school and department crisis teams.

Operational debriefing procedure

(1) Introduction
   o State the purpose of the debriefing.
   o State the ground rules.

(2) Facts of the incident
   o Participants gain consensus on what happened.
   o Participants gain consensus on the order things happened.
   o Describe the role of each team member.

(3) Assessment of the intervention
   o Review the team performance.
   o Acknowledge things done well.

o   Identify areas for improvement.

(4)   Reactions

o   Discuss individual reactions during the incident.

(5)   Interpretation of response

o   Take the opportunity to make sense of the incident from a professional perspective.

o   Provide a chance to understand the incident.

(6)   Plans for improvement

o   Identify lessons learned for future crisis response.

(7)   Closing

o   Make plans to implement the lessons learned from the current incident.

ONGOING STUDENT COUNSELING

Most of the work in the aftermath of a crisis will fall upon the shoulders of the school's counselor. Invite anyone who wishes to participate to attend a group (six to eight students) once or twice for counseling and discussion of the incident. Students who are particularly at risk due to the crisis should be referred to a group. Some students may also require individual sessions if their problems are different from those of the other students, or if they are so upset that their participation in a group may intensify the reactions of the other group members.

EVALUATING THE CRISIS RESPONSE PLAN

Once the crisis is over and things have returned to normal, it is important to evaluate the crisis response plan. If you do not conduct an evaluation you will not know if the plan was successful or if it made a difference. Evaluating the crisis plan on an annual basis will provide a degree of quality assurance to the plan. When evaluating the plan ask such questions as:

- Was the plan effective? Why? Why not?

- Was responsibility evenly distributed?

- Was there any effect on staff members who have traumatic events in their past?

- Was additional support requested from the District/Division? Why? Why not?

- Did the incident require crisis intervention or emergency support?

- What parts of the plan worked smoothly? Why?

- Which parts of the plan did not work well? Why?

- What needs to be changed for the next time?

Gathering feedback about the crisis response plan

There are three sources of information you can access when evaluating the crisis intervention plan. The following may be helpful in guiding your information gathering.

Gathering feedback from students

- Did the plan help them in dealing with the incident?
- Did they learn alternative strategies for dealing with the incident?

Gathering feedback from the community

- Are children coping with the incident?
- Were children willing to talk about the incident to parents?
- Were parents aware that swift and positive action was being taken by the school to deal with the incident?

Gathering feedback from all school staff

- How did they feel about their responsibilities?
- Were they able to handle it?
- What would they like to see changed in the plan?
- How can the plan be improved?

WHAT TO DO

Step 9: Respond appropriately to specific types of crises

RESPONDING TO VIOLENCE

In the twenty-first century, violence and conflict are always with us. We all witness death and tragedy on television and on social media. Sometimes violence and conflict impact our own lives. Mass shootings, stabbings, random attacks, sexual assaults and fights can occur in any school, in any community. No one is immune. We all live with that fear. One way to deal with the anxiety that violence will touch your school is to consider what you need to do if it should happen.

Any violent incident will affect the educational process and reduce its effectiveness. Students who either experience violence directly or indirectly have increased anxiety and fear that will affect their academic performance and commitment to education. An overall safety plan for crisis intervention requires a thoughtful process for identifying security needs, developing intervention and prevention techniques, evaluating physical facilities, and providing communication between students and staff.

Typical waves of response to a violent crisis

When a violent crisis does occur, it is of utmost importance to have an effective crisis intervention plan. The immediate aftereffect of a violent crisis produces three waves of reaction that can overwhelm staff and existing resources.

(1) **Police and rescue workers will arrive.** Police will make decisions regarding student and staff safety, disarm the situation, and start their investigation. They may order a lockdown of the school.

(2) **The media will arrive.** Members of the media will not give up because of the high impact of violence. They will do their best to get the story. Follow the guidelines for handling the media (see Step 4, and Appendix 2). When responding to media questions, try to help them answer the questions of what happened, where, when, why and how. Inform them if anyone has been hurt or if no one is hurt. Also, tell them if and how the police are involved in the situation.

(3) **Anxious parents will either begin to arrive at the school or flood the school with telephone calls.** Be prepared to answer calls.

o   Ask parents to please do not attempt to come to the school if Police are not allowing people in the school.

o   Advise them the school will notify them when and where they can pick up their child.

o   Tell them the media will keep them informed as to when and where they can pick up their children.

Possible levels of police intervention

It should be noted that before requesting direct police intervention, every effort to settle a disruption should be made by school staff. The police department should be notified of the school disturbance as a matter of record and reference for any future need for assistance. School and police officials respond to disturbance in accordance to the level of intensity. The three levels of intensity are:

- **Level 1: No direct police intervention** - The disturbance is confined to one area and without threat to students or staff. School personnel respond by containing or removing persons involved with minimum interruption.

- **Level 2: Direct police intervention** - The disturbance is mobile and/or poses a direct threat to students and staff. The school remains open, but police officers isolate the disruptive activity, detain individuals involved, and terminate the threat of escalation. As many school personnel, as possible should carry out routine school operations during the disturbance.

- **Level 3: Direct police intervention** - The disturbance prevents regular school operations from continuing. There are serious threats to students and staff safety, and the situation is no longer within the school's control. The principal requests police assistance in accordance with guidelines previously established in a written memorandum of understanding between police officials and the principal and/or school division/district. Police officers at the scene close or lock down the school and assume responsibility for controlling the situation. Authority to end the disruption shifts from the principal and/or area superintendent to the police officer in charge. Responsibility for maintaining safety and order among students and staff, and responsibility for the facility remain with the school's principal and area superintendent.

Conducting a situational assessment after a violent incident

If an act of violence creates a crisis in the school, the principal should conduct a situational assessment prior to police intervention.

Questions to ask when conducting this assessment should include:

- Is the school safe and secure for the students?

- Is there a need to call in police officers?

- Who witnessed the incident?

- Are the witnesses likely to be traumatized?

- Are there any legal issues that could affect the crisis response team or school?

- Which classes are likely to be affected the most?

- Are there staff members who may be affected more than others?

- Are rival gangs or groups at the school involved?

- Is discipline or crowd control going to be a problem?

- Which groups are likely to be affected?

- Are there any historical, social, personal, or cultural factors that may affect the situation?

Preparing for police involvement

It is important to have specific procedures established involving the police responding to violence or a violent crisis at the school. These procedures should be developed in cooperation with the appropriate police officials, school principal, and area superintendent.

(1) Declare an emergency (generally done by the principal) and request assistance through direct communication with the area superintendent.

(2) Establish a predetermined Emergency Operations Center (EOC) where the principal or area superintendent works with emergency services and clearly defines the responsibilities of each person.

(3) Establish emergency procedures that include notifying local law enforcement agencies, the fire department, and medical assistance agencies as appropriate. In some communities, law enforcement officials handle contacts with other agencies in the event of an emergency.

(4) Post and regularly update a list of emergency telephone numbers in the staff room.

Enabling and maintaining effective communication

Another important component of any crisis plan is a procedure that enables effective communication with all school staff and external agencies that may be assisting in the management of a critical incident.

(1) Establish a clear communication system that signals an emergency, and when the crisis has passed, signals an "all clear." The signal should be distinguishable from those that designate class periods, and should be established prior to an emergency.

(2) Establish a rumor control/information post in a location accessible to parents, interested community members, and media, to handle inquiries in an orderly fashion. This post would provide a system for swift parental contact and an outside line for specific communications to community transportation volunteers.

(3) Have the principal act as the police contact person for the school.

(4)   Designate a spokesperson to advise the media and respond to questions and concerns.

(5)   Develop a procedure for establishing and maintaining control of the media and onlookers who could impede operations. Have the school district/division's communications team provide updated information on the status of a crisis at regular intervals to minimize rumors and interruptions.

(6)   Develop procedures for keeping family members and other relatives informed about students enrolled in the school.

(7)   Select a person for taking messages and recording incidents for documentation purposes.

(8)   Establish a system for message delivery and backup in case initial communications break down.

(9)   After the crisis has subsided and students have been dismissed, debrief all staff members about the emergency and the procedures taken.

Safety considerations during/after a violent incident

During any incident involving violence, it is critical that all staff and students are safe from further trauma and other sources of potential danger.

Address the safety considerations listed below BEFORE a crisis occurs, and conduct periodic practice drills to ensure that procedures for dismissal run smoothly.

(1)   Devise a signal for announcing an emergency. This signal may differ depending on the type of emergency and available devices.

(2)   Identify who can declare an emergency and under what conditions. The principal should make this decision.

(3)   Develop a procedure for identifying safe and injured students.

(4)   Identify an adequate location and a procedure for administering first aid.

(5)   Develop a systematic process for releasing students to parents or guardians that includes a sign-out procedure and verification of persons authorized to pick up students. Provide a description of the process in other languages for non-English speaking parents.

(6)   Establish a "clean up" committee to be called in immediately following a disaster to completely clean and to repair damages so that the school can open as soon as the following day. Identify possible professional non-school personnel to do the clean-up, especially in the event of gunshot victims.

(7)   Identify a crisis intervention team of psychologists and counselors to be called to provide debriefing and counseling for any resulting trauma affecting students and staff members.

(8)   Establish an orderly dismissal procedure; e.g., dismissal by floors or sections, in a manner that everyone understands.

(9) Provide parents with information in their first language, if possible, regarding relevant elements of the emergency plan, so they are prepared and know what to expect.

(10) Establish a "buddy system" for all students, especially significantly disabled students.

Procedure for dealing with a violent/potentially violent individual

During any violent crisis intervention, the safety of crisis response team members is a serious concern. To ensure that every attempt is made to maintain personal safety, observe the following procedures when conducting counseling, defusing, or debriefing sessions with potentially violent students while in the counselor's office, classroom, or other office.

(1) Conduct the interview with a partner, if possible. Never remain after school hours with a violent student unless you have a partner.

(2) Remove any potential weapons (e.g. heavy ashtray, letter opener, paperweight etc.) from the immediate environment where you will meet with the individual.

(3) Know where your phone or the nearest available telephone is located.

(4) Know your potential exit areas.

(5) When greeting the individual, notice anything strange about his or her words, behavior, or dress.

    o Conduct a visual frisk.

    o Note the individual's body language.

(6) Attempt to speak with the individual at eye level. Avoid standing over the individual. If the person chooses to remain standing, do the same.

    o Position the individual next to the door.

    o Never position yourself in a corner. There is no escape there.

    o If sitting, sit with your feet flat on the floor with your hands unfolded in your lap and lean slightly forward. This conveys interest and concern and also allows you to respond immediately if you are threatened physically.

    o If standing, have your feet about shoulder width apart, one foot slightly behind the other, and weight on the rear leg, knees slightly bent, with hands folded but not interlocked.

(7) Inform the individual that you have a partner in the outer office.

(8) Be prepared for unexpected behavior.

    o Frequently ask yourself "what if" this happens.

    o Never turn your back on a violent individual or allow them to walk behind you.

RESPONDING TO THREATS

Due to the increase in terrorism and violence in schools, departments of education and school administrations have been encouraged to develop multidisciplinary teams to conduct threat assessments and risk assessments.

Threat assessment is the process of collecting data through structured interviews to determine the level of risk that may be posed by a threat maker against a target or multiple targets and plan an appropriate strategy to reduce the potential risk to the target or targets.

Types of threats

There are four types of threats: direct threats, indirect threats, veiled threats, and conditional threats.

Direct and indirect threats

Direct threats are verbalized, written, or gestured, and indicate direct action to be taken against one or more individuals, an object or building.

Indirect threats are verbalized or written and suggest that an action will be taken against one or more individuals, an object or building.

The difference between direct and indirect is that an indirect threat is not clearly indicated but is implied.

Veiled threats

Veiled threats are not as clear in terms of language. The threat can be cloaked with ambiguity in terms of the intended action. Veiled threats may be uttered against one or more individuals or an object or building.

Conditional threats

Conditional threats are uttered as an ultimatum if some other intended action or condition is not met to the satisfaction of the threat maker.

Assessing risk

Although the belief that the best predictor of future behavior is past behavior, there are a few problems with this view. First, many people engage in violent behavior but never come close to becoming murderers. Second, many individuals who have turned guns and knives on others had no history of violence prior to the act of becoming murderers. These individuals have been called "empty vessels" due to the lack of connection many had to healthy mature adults as well as their lack of clear identity, place, or purpose.

Risk assessment is the process of determining if an individual previously identified through the threat assessment process poses a risk to a target or targets identified by the individual under investigation. In most cases, the individual has not actually threatened to kill a target or targets but his or her behavior or thoughts have been increasingly violent, suggesting that the potential for violence may be escalating.

Responsibility to report potentially high-risk behaviors

Any person in a school having knowledge of high-risk behavior or having reasonable grounds to believe there is a potential for high-risk behavior shall promptly report the information to the school principal (Cameron, 2004).

No action will be taken against a person who makes a report unless the report is made maliciously and without reasonable grounds. In such cases, the person making the malicious report shall be dealt with according to the department of education or district policy, where applicable.

Possible levels of response after risk assessment

There are four levels of response that may result from the information gathered by the multidisciplinary threat assessment team. The level of response implemented by an administrator is in reaction to the perceived or anticipated level of risk indicated by a threat maker. These four levels can be categorized as immediate risk situations, threat making behaviors, worrisome behaviors, and exceptional high-profile worrisome behaviors.

Response to immediate risk situations

Immediate risk situations are those situations that include armed intruders inside the building or on the periphery who may pose an immediate risk to a target or targets. The school principal should immediately contact the police and take the necessary steps to ensure the safety of all students and staff.

Response to threat-making behaviors

Threat-making behaviors are behaviors exhibited by high school students who utter, convey or cause any person to receive a threat of death or bodily harm. If a threat has been made, the school principal should immediately contact the police, and take the necessary steps to ensure the safety of all students and staff.

Response to worrisome behaviors

Worrisome behaviors are those behaviors (or a threat maker) that cause concern for members of the school administration or divisional/district office personnel. These behaviors indicate or suggest that the threat maker is, or may be, moving toward a greater risk of violent behavior. Most threat-related behaviors from children in kindergarten to twelfth grade fall into this category. When students utter generalized threats, the principal should contact the school psychologist or counselor for a consultation to determine if the information or incident warrants further action.

Note: Students (pre-teens and older) who threaten others may have committed a criminal offence. The threat may be criminal in most jurisdictions whether the student threatened another student, or a teacher or administrator. In these cases, the school principal or another responsible adult should contact the police and take the steps needed to ensure the safety of all students and staff.

Response to high-profile worrisome behaviors

High-profile worrisome behaviors occur in settings where there is an audience that may already be traumatized, and whose reactions to the incident may trigger a broader trauma response within the school or community. These situations may arise due to elevated sensitivity by some students, staff, or parents in the aftermath of high-profile traumatic events, such as school shootings or other violent incidents.

Writing a threat-assessment report

Following a threat assessment, a threat assessment report should be written. This report is usually written by the principal in collaboration with team members. Its contents should include the following, adapted from the "Guide for preventing and responding to school violence" (International Association of Chiefs of Police).

- name of the threat maker and his or her relationship to the school and recipient
- name of the target or potential targets
- when and where the incident occurred
- what happened immediately prior to the incident
- the specific language of the threat
- physical conduct that would support intent to follow through on a threat
- how the threat maker appeared emotionally and physically
- names of others who were directly involved and any actions they took
- how the incident ended
- names of any witnesses
- description of what happened to the threat maker after the incident
- description of what happened to other directly involved individuals after the incident
- names of any administrators, teachers, or staff and how they responded
- any history leading up to the event
- steps that have been taken to ensure the threat will not be carried out
- suggestions for preventing school violence in the future

RESPONDING TO SUICIDE

Suicide is not triggered by the mere mention of the word and preparing for response to a suicide does not denote expectation of a suicide. A willingness to deal openly with issues related to suicide, along with planning appropriate help and support, aims at preventing and minimizing its devastating consequences.

Preventing suicide

A program that focuses on prevention should seek to help teachers and counselors identify the broad spectrum of "at risk" students. Curriculum on prevention should focus on development of coping skills, identification of depression, coping with depression, problem-solving techniques, decision-making strategies, and stress management.

Knowing the risk factors for suicide

Suicide risk factors include:

- a sense of not belonging in a school
- a sense of having a restricted future because of doing poorly in school
- alienation from peers
- a low level of family support

Environmental factors in the school that may increase the risk of suicide include:

- recent transitions imposed by the system
- lack of specialized programs
- a social climate with strong cliques and factions
- alienation and rejection of certain students
- excess attention given to suicide threats or attempts

Identifying and intervening with "at-risk" individuals

At times a crisis team member may be called upon to intervene with a student or group of students identified as "at risk" for suicide. Keep in mind that there is no right or wrong way to intervene with a suicidal individual.

It is critical to assess everyone. Consult with those who initially identified the individual "at risk." Gather background information and social history, as well as identify family members, situational factors, and any behavioral signs that might be warning signs of potential suicide.

Remember that your assessment will provide an estimate of the degree of risk only. Interpretation of that risk should be made very conservatively (i.e., err on the side of suicide potential).

Potential suicide warning signs

Warning signs of potential suicide include the following.

- The person is preoccupied with the thoughts of death, and exhibits any of the following signs:
    - a specific plan for a suicide attempt
    - the means to carry out the suicide act
    - suicide threats, notes, or repeated statements about his or her death
    - a previous suicide attempt
    - the death of a significant person through suicide
    - making final arrangements, such as giving favored things away, writing a will, putting relationships in order
    - sudden apparent resolution of difficulties manifests as calmness, indicating suicide as a solution

- The person has experienced significant (possibly recent) changes in relationships and environment, such as:
    - loss of a significant person through death, divorce, or separation
    - loss of an object of affection
    - loss of employment, of financial security, of status
    - loss of health, in the form of serious illness or chronic pain
    - geographical move or school change

- The person exhibits observable changes in motivation and behavior, including:
    - decreased work or academic performance
    - persistent lateness or unexplained absences from work or school
    - decreased social activity, isolation, aloofness, withdrawal
    - apparent loss of involvement in interests and hobbies
    - aggressiveness, moodiness, lethargy, not communicating
    - evidence of anxiousness, extreme tension, agitation, restlessness
    - lack of concentration, preoccupation
    - outbursts of anger at self and/or the world
    - self-abuse
    - physical mutilation or other self-inflicted injury
    - taking unwarranted risks
    - substance abuse

- The person shows observable changes in emotional disposition and personality, such as:

- o self-dislike ("I hate myself" / "I'm no good")
- o feeling hopeless and helpless
- o feeling misunderstood and unappreciated
- o signs of severe mental depression
- o cries easily
- o communication that life is too painful or difficult
- o loss of pleasure
- The person exhibits physical/somatic changes, such as:
  - o loss of or increase in appetite; weight change
  - o increase or decrease in sleep
  - o exhaustion
  - o loss of physical or mental energy
  - o inability to experience pleasure
- The person appears to be under significant stress, due to:
  - o personal loss
  - o sexual assault
  - o abuse

Determining level of risk

When dealing with an individual who may be suicidal it is very important to determine the level of risk that person presents in terms of attempting suicide. If you ask directly, you will know whether the person has thoughts about suicide.

In addition, there are three factors that are used as predictors of the immediate risk of suicide:

- prior suicidal behavior
- a current suicide plan
- few internal and external resources

Remember to take all threats seriously.

The "PCRT" assessment for determining level of risk

Ramsay, Tanney, Tierney, and Lang (1994) developed information for determining level of suicide risk, as outlined below.

P - PRIOR SUICIDAL BEHAVIOR

- Has the individual tried suicide before? If yes, the risk is higher.

- Is there a history of suicide in the immediate family? If yes, the risk is higher.

Summary:

- *Previous attempts*
- *Family history of suicidal behavior*

C - CURRENT SUICIDE PLAN

- How the individual plans to do it. Does he or she have a weapon or means to complete the act? The more lethal the method, the more likely the death will occur.

- Is the individual prepared to do it? Has he or she made specific plans and preparations to complete the act?

- When will it happen? Is there a specific time, or how close to the time is it now?

Summary:

- *specific plan - the more specific the plan, the higher the risk*
- *access to lethal means - the more lethal the means, the higher the risk*
- *has completed preparations - the more complete the preparations, the higher the risk*
- *specific time - the closer the time, the higher the risk*

R - RESOURCES, INTERNAL AND EXTERNAL

- internal resources:
  - high self-esteem and high self-confidence
  - positive outlook on life
  - realistic goals and dreams
  - good physical and mental health
  - good employment skills
- external resources:
  - many friends
  - healthy family
  - stable home
  - positive role models to follow
  - access to professional help
  - satisfying job/academic career

Summary

- *the fewer internal and external resources, the higher the risk*

T - TAKE ALL THREATS SERIOUSLY!

102

Suicide contagion and suicide clusters: A research overview

A large portion of suicide research supports the notion that suicide is socially contagious in that it causes imitation (Gould et al., 2003). This contagion can, purportedly, lead to suicide clusters. Suicide clusters can be an extremely unfortunate result of a student suicide. Suicide clusters are difficult to combat and should be of great concern to the crisis team. The Centers for Disease Control (CDC) define suicide clusters "as a group of suicides or suicide attempts, or both, that occur closer together in time and space than would normally be expected in a given community" (1988, pp. 1). Cox et al. found six main approaches that schools and communities adopt for the attempted reduction and eradication of suicide clusters (2012). They are as follows:

> *Development of a community response plan; educational/psychological debriefings; providing both individual and group counseling to affected peers; screening of high-risk individuals; responsible media reporting of the suicide cluster; and promotion of health recovery within the community to prevent future suicides. (p. 209)*

Cox et al. found that these approaches did not yield significant evidence for effectiveness across the literature, although some studies do show promise (2012). More research on suicide clusters and their prevention is needed.

Responding to assessed risk

When the assessed risk is high

- Make a contract with the suicidal person that he or she will not harm him-/herself (see below).
- Do not leave the person alone and don't allow him or her to leave a safe place. Assign a staff member to maintain visual contact always.
- Contact parents.
- Inform the student and parents of what has been done.
- Contact mental health services/social services/police immediately.
- Remove all dangerous articles from the environment.
- Consider hospitalization or having the individual legally committed to hospital.
- Have the individual "at risk" develop a survival kit (see below).

When the assessed risk is low:

- Identify positive traits.
- Understand negative feelings.
- Point out that suicide is a permanent solution to a short-term problem.
- Attempt to help reduce stress.
- Inform the student and parents what has been done.

- Set short-term realistic goals.

- Build a support network.

- Negotiate a contract with the student; ask them to promise to seek further help and to not harm themselves

- Point out other resources.

- Strengthen existing coping skills and abilities.

- Have the individual at risk develop a survival kit (see below).

Creating a suicide prevention survival kit

The act of assembling a survival kit by a potential suicide victim is a strong message that he or she is willing to stand up to the thoughts of suicide and take active steps toward preserving life and future.

The individual does not have to wait until all problems are solved to assemble the kit. He or she should do it now. The simple act of planning for survival can awaken a renewed sense of personal worth and hopefulness in the individual. Assembling the survival kit will also remind the individual that he or she values life enough to prepare for the difficult times.

The contents of the kit should contain items that are important to the individual, and will vary from one person to another. Some ideas are suggested below.

- pictures of the person's family or other loved ones (of those for whom it is important to go on living)

- letters written to the person by loved ones

- a letter written by the person to him- or herself as a reminder of all the things that are valuable and worth living for

- a few small cherished items

- a small teapot and a bag of tea to remind the person to make a cup of tea before taking any action that may cause harm

- a chocolate bar or whatever is the person's favorite treat

- a tape of favorite songs that is long enough to distract until any self-destructive thoughts pass

- books of poems or mediations that might help the person to regain perspective

- objects that support the person's spiritual perspective (e.g., a Bible with passages marked), or some other spiritual resources that can help the person through a difficult time

- a telephone list of people that the person trusts and to whom the person can turn for help and support

- a list of telephone numbers for the local distress line and local hospital

Creating a suicide prevention contract

Another strategy that a helper may take with a person thinking about committing suicide is to develop a contract with the individual. Contracts may appeal to the troubled individual's sense of fairness and the reliability of his or her word.

The contract is a brief document that spells out in clear terms what the suicidal individual will do if he or she makes a decision to attempt to commit suicide within a specific period. If the person feels the urge to attempt suicide, he/she agrees to contact a person or persons identified in the contract. Both the helper and the troubled individual sign and date the contract.

The contents of a contract may vary depending on the situation and individual(s). Both signatories should have a copy of the signed contract. The troubled individual should be encouraged to keep a copy with them always. A sample contract is included below.

Sample suicide prevention contract

I, _____, agree that I will not attempt to commit suicide or hurt myself in any way for the next _____ days.

If I feel that I will try to break this contract and I am at school, I will immediately contact _____ at _____.

If I feel that I will try to break this contract and I am not at school, I will immediately contact _____ at _____.

I agree that I will not make any final decision or attempt at committing suicide until I have talked with my counselor/helper directly.

This contract is effective immediately.

_____   _____

Student   *Date*

_____   _____

Counselor   *Date*

Strategies for interviewing a suicidal individual

Ramsay, Tanney, Tierney, and Lang (1994) stress that when interviewing a client who is suicidal it is important to accomplish the following:

(1) Engage the individual. Use appropriate attending skills when speaking and listening.

(2) Identify whether the individual is thinking about suicide. Ask directly: "Are you thinking about committing suicide?"

(3) Inquire as to the reasons behind the intention of suicide. What is motivating this person to consider suicide?

(4) Make your assessment using the PCRT assessment (as developed by Ramsay, R., Tanney, B., Tierney, R., and Lang, W., 1994).

(5) Negotiate a suicide prevention contract with the individual. Both you and the suicidal person must be working toward the same goal.

(6) Develop a suicide prevention survival kit.

(7) Follow through on whatever you and the individual have agreed upon.

Things to remember

- Most individuals will exhibit warning signs that they are contemplating suicide.

- Talking and asking direct questions about suicide will not increase the risk.

- Suicidal individuals tend to be confused as to whether they want to die or not.

- If a person attempts suicide and fails, he or she may try again. Most do not. Some do.

- When someone has been depressed but then comes out of the depression, the danger is not yet over.

- Unsuccessful or non-fatal attempts at suicide are not attention getting strategies. They are cries for help.

- Suicide is not a response that has little thought behind it. Most suicide victims have planned the event over time.

- Individuals should be reminded that suicide is not an alternative for problem solving. It is a permanent solution to short-term difficulties.

- Suicidal individuals cannot see any alternatives for themselves.

The link between uncompleted and completed suicide

It is most important for crisis team members to understand the link between uncompleted suicide and completed suicides. There are four possible motivations that may be associated with non-fatal attempted suicides:

- **attachment** - Attachment issues may be associated with loss of a partner in a relationship or an attempt to change the existing one.

- **escape** - Escape may be associated with circumstances in the individual's life that are too difficult to bear (e.g. chronic pain, depression, or illness).

- **control** - Control may represent an attempt to exert control over someone else.

- **release** - Release may be an attempt to eliminate or reduce personal, physical or psychological pressure.

Team members should note that the intent of non-fatal suicidal behavior is not necessarily death. It is a strong cry for help.

After a suicide has occurred

After a completed suicide has occurred, family, friends and colleagues are concerned with trying to cope with the loss. An additional concern is the possibility of more tragedy. Often it has been the view that a suicide recognized by way of a memorial service, tribute, or intervention may encourage copycat suicide attempts. There is no research to support this view.

It is important to avoid long-term memorializing that may appear to glorify and romanticize the event. Holding a special day, event, or naming something in memory of the deceased is not a recommended practice, as it may suggest to others that the choice of suicide was a good one.

It is important to encourage thinking that reinforces the idea that other choices and options would have been a more effective way to deal with the problems.

The absence of a response by the school will only drive the discussion underground. Parents and staff are advised to help children work through their questions and fears.

Students and/or staff who may have come upon the scene or were witnesses to the act may be seriously traumatized. These individuals should be seen apart from the rest of the student body. The event will have a far more serious effect on these individuals. It is most important to identify those students who may be most at risk due to a completed suicide, including:

- individuals who were especially close to the deceased
- siblings or relatives
- close friends and those who felt they were confidants to the deceased
- individuals who express extreme signs of grief and guilt over the incident
- individuals who have attempted suicide in the past
- individuals with significant personal problems who feel their problems cannot be resolved
- individuals who have recently lost a significant member of their family
- individuals who feel responsible for the death ("I should have known" or "I should have done something, it's my fault")

Remember to record the date of the event. This anniversary date will have significance next year when many students remember the initial incident.

RESPONDING TO SUDDEN LOSS

As a crisis team member, you may be called to respond to a traumatic event that involves both the permanent loss of an individual by death and the temporary loss of an individual from the community due to incarceration.

For example, a motor vehicle accident occurs and one individual is killed and the other individual is not, but the unharmed person has contributed to the death of the first person in some way (e.g. impaired driving or negligence). You must deal with the feelings and emotions surrounding the precipitating event (the critical incident) associated with the loss and grief over the death. And you also need to deal with the feelings and emotions from the loss of the unharmed individual if he or she will be removed from the school community, or even incarcerated, because of his or her actions.

Debriefing

These difficult situations often create conflicting feelings and tend to polarize groups of students and community members. The response should focus first on dealing with the critical incident and conducting the debriefing. The debriefings should follow the outlines presented earlier in this book. Individuals closest to both victims should be debriefed individually.

Common responses to sudden loss

It is important to note that regression is a common response to loss. The more serious and sudden the loss, the more the individual's cycle of distress, coping abilities, and withdrawal may resemble acute traumatic stress.

Another response to sudden loss may be acute grief response. Individuals experiencing acute grief response are completely incapacitated. Conducting individual and classroom debriefings will be helpful. It is important to assess individual functioning, safety needs, and available support.

RESPONDING WHEN A CHILD IS TERMINALLY ILL

It is possible that you may have a student in your class who is terminally ill. Often questions arise about the individual because he or she may have undergone obvious physical changes, missed a significant amount of time from school, or been too weak to participate in various school activities. Classmates may start to ask difficult questions about the child. The teacher may not know how to answer the students' questions.

Firstly, keep in mind that it is important for the sick child to be in school. Children who are terminally ill still want to learn, play, and be with friends. Second, parents tend to hang on to hope so tightly that the school may be unable to prepare classmates for the eventual death of their peer.

The question is how do you prepare classmates? Medical information is confidential and cannot be discussed in class or elsewhere unless the parent or parents have given written permission. Efforts should be made to obtain parental permission to discuss the subjects with classmates.

If permission is not granted there are a few things the classroom teacher can do to help prepare the other students. Listed below are some suggestions, as presented by Petersen and Straub (1992):

- Ensure that the sick child is not in the classroom at the time of the discussion, to reduce that child's stress and anxiety. Also, having the sick child present will tend to hamper the discussion.

- Try to determine what other classmates have noticed about the child that sets him or her apart from the others.

- Gradually introduce the fact that the child is seriously ill.

- Solicit views from other students about the illness. This gives the teacher a reference as to how classmates understand and interpret their peer's behavior and condition.

- Inform the class about the child's illness. It is important that other students understand that they cannot catch this illness. You will likely have to repeat several times that others cannot catch the illness.

- Next, tell the others what will happen to their classmate.

- At this point it is important to tell the students what they can do to help make things easier or happier for their classmate.

- Remember that elementary students need to be reminded more often than junior and senior high school students.

- Keep in mind that children are often aware that one of their peers may be quite different from them. This may not be a source of concern for them. In other words, "if it isn't broken, don't try to fix it."

RESPONDING TO A FAMILY CRISIS

In most instances, it is not the responsibility of school-based crisis teams to respond to family crises. However, it is helpful, and indeed important, for helpers to understand the home situation of students exhibiting signs and symptoms of either acute traumatic stress or acute grief response. All students need a strong support system at home. Students coming from families that are experiencing some form of crisis likely do not have much in the way of support at home.

Families experiencing some form of crisis may exhibit these behavioral signs (Steel and Raider (1991):

- emotionally cool, detached, and aloof

- emotionally explosive and unpredictable

- unwilling to communicate

- unwilling to ask for help or accept it

- closed to different ways of coping

- absence of family in decision making

- denial, withdrawal, or avoidance of inherent conflicts within a crisis

- loss of parental direction, guidance, and support

- substance abuse

- scapegoating and blaming

RESPONDING TO A LARGE-SCALE DISASTER

Large-scale or natural disasters affect the entire community. Such disasters include earthquakes, floods, fires, hurricanes, tsunamis, tornadoes, etc. The effects of a natural disaster are community-wide and cause tremendous destruction. The damage is sudden and irreversible. People feel isolated.

Should such an event take place, the appropriate school response is outlined in the **Large-scale disaster checklist** in Appendix 2. This is particularly important, since when a crisis affects everyone (such as in a large scale disaster), panic may set in, memory is short-circuited, and tasks are often done in a haphazard manner.

Factors that affect recovery

Recovery from natural disasters tends to be more difficult than recovering from critical incidents involving the death of an individual. Recovery is inhibited by the nature of the widespread destruction and the lack of personal control experienced by individuals.

Other factors that affect recovery include the loss of personal possessions, inadequate financial resources, and possibly, inaccurate reporting by the press. Also, during a natural disaster there may be looting and loss of communication with other areas.

Effects on school-aged children

School-aged children who experience natural or large-scale disasters experience similar reactions as those during other crises. The predominant reaction by elementary school children tends to be fear. Fear is exhibited by a general sense of anxiety, hyperactivity, and flashbacks. There may an increase in the number of stomach illnesses and headaches. During a disaster adolescents tend to miss more school and there may also be an increase in substance abuse. It is important to note that these emotions are easily rekindled by associative factors that remind the victims of the original disaster.

RESPONDING TO A MARINE DISASTER

Sometimes students can be involved in a marine disaster while traveling or on a field trip. Marine disasters that involve numerous passengers or large ships are rarely an accident. Almost invariably they are the consequence of a chain of events. The removal of any one link will prevent the disaster occurring or at least mitigate the outcome. A well prepared, effective disaster plan will be the very last link in that chain, and the only chance to ensure that a bad situation does not get worse simply because of a lack of planning.

Special difficulties associated with marine disasters

Marine disasters can be especially difficult and dangerous due to water conditions such as temperature, wave height, location, and the presence of other potentially dangerous materials on the vessel. Marine disasters may also involve discharge of oil or other dangerous pollutants into the environment.

Response to marine disasters

Marine disasters involve many different responders. Traditionally, the military has been responsible for conducting search and rescue operations. If an aircraft goes down at sea, the civil aviation authority will also be involved.

If there is concern about dangerous pollutants leaking into the sea, specialized teams or agencies trained to conduct clean up and recovery will be involved. The rescue of large numbers of people at sea or in open water is slow unless other ships are close by. Coordination and cooperation between governments and organizations is imperative to launch a successful rescue operation.

WHAT TO DO

Step 10: Develop (or amend) a school crisis plan for the future

DEVELOP A COMPREHENSIVE CRISIS PLAN – OR REVIEW YOUR EXISTING PLAN

We have discussed various strategies and procedures that will help you prepare for a crisis and deal with one that has occurred. The next sections provide a summary of what you need to do.

Determine a single entry/exit

Establishing one location to enter and exit the school enables school staff to prevent seriously distraught students from leaving the building unescorted or without parental permission. A single entry and exit also enables staff to better determine who is in the building.

Set up a crisis center

It is most helpful if a specific room can be set up as the crisis center. This is where all the work, strategy sessions, and planning during the critical incident will take place. The room should be equipped with a chalk or white board, large table, chairs, coffee machine, and a dedicated crisis telephone line. The room should be private and not normally accessed by staff or visitors to the school, so the traditional staff room is not a good location for the crisis center. Staff debriefings may be done here, so keep lots of tissue on hand for use during these debriefings.

Create a student drop-in center

This strategy is used when a critical incident affects a junior/senior high school. The drop-in center is often set up in the school library (as this tends to be a quiet place), and is staffed by either two counselors or teaching staff. The drop-in center is set up the first day. The drop-in center is a quiet place where students can go when they wish to be alone or are having difficulty coping in the classroom. All teachers and staff should be told that students may go to the center at any time. Permission is not needed, but students should notify the teacher about where they are going. Defusing sessions and group discussions may take place in the drop-in center.

Set up a media center

If a critical incident develops into a lengthy one, it is helpful to set up a separate room as a media center, where journalists can interview the school's spokesperson, etc. The media center should be equipped with tables, chairs, telephones, computers, a photocopier, coffee/tea dispenser, and a white or chalk board. This is where scheduled meetings with individual reporters may be held, and where journalists can work. You may also need a space to deal with larger groups of media (for making announcements, etc.)

Defuse emotions

Conducting defusing sessions is one of the first attempts to help individuals start to face the critical incident. Students may be angry, hostile and extremely emotional. The procedure used in defusing emotions is unstructured, and usually is begun during the first day of an incident. Counselors and crisis team members most often conduct these sessions. Teachers familiar with the process may conduct defusing sessions as well. Defusing sessions are usually limited to eight to ten individuals.

Offer group debriefing

Group discussion usually takes place after things have started to calm down (typically during the second day). Group debriefings follow a semi-structured format, and may be facilitated by a counselor, crisis team member, or teacher familiar with the procedure. Group debriefings represent the first step in helping individuals put the incident and their reactions in perspective. Debriefing groups should be limited to approximately fourteen individuals. Although students may be angry and in denial, they may also show some signs of acceptance.

Offer solution-focused counseling

The solution-focused approach to counseling is mentioned here because it tends to be quite effective. Its success may be attributed, in part, to the fact that the solutions are student-generated and focus on what the individual is doing correctly. Trained counselors or crisis team members usually implement this process. Sessions are conducted on an individual basis and may be utilized throughout and for some, after a critical incident. The students may exhibit a full range of emotions.

Offer individual debriefing

The individual debriefing procedure follows a semi-structured format. Individual debriefings are usually implemented during the first two days of a critical incident, as a more formal attempt to help the individuals deal with the critical incident. This is the most appropriate way to debrief those individuals who were closest to the victim, felt they were responsible for the death, or believe could have prevented it. The students may exhibit a full range of emotions.

Offer classroom debriefing

Classroom debriefings provide an opportunity to present to a larger group the facts as they are known and clarify any misinformation. The format is structured and conducted by the counselor, crisis team member, or teacher familiar with the procedure. Debriefings are usually started on the first day of a critical incident and follow into the second day. Classroom debriefings vary in length, but usually do not last longer than thirty to forty-five minutes. Reactions during a debriefing tend to be much more subdued when compared with individual sessions.

Consider a healing circle

Native Americans sometimes use this procedure when dealing with a critical incident. The format tends to be unstructured. Healing circles are used to help individuals deal with the incident and understand their feelings. Use of a familiar object to identify the person speaking is important. This procedure usually occurs during the first two days. Healing circles may be implemented in a classroom. These sessions are conducted by a Native American elder, counselor, crisis team member, or teachers familiar with the procedure. Healing circles may last between forty-five to ninety minutes.

Appoint hall monitors

Specific staff persons are assigned to patrol the halls and washrooms to ensure that students are not gathering in large groups. This is an attempt to keep students who are less affected by the incident from becoming significantly influenced by the emotionality of those closest to the victim. This tends to be more necessary at the junior and senior grade level as adolescents tend to feed off the emotional reactions of those in an emotionally fragile state. Hall monitors are used during the first two or three days of the incident. Monitors can watch for any signs of shrines or other such symbols being made of the victim's desk or locker. This is especially important if a critical incident is due to suicide.

Draft an information letter

This is a letter prepared and sent out by the principal. It is prepared the first day and sent home with every student at school. It contains specific information to help parents assist their child in dealing with the incident. The letter should also state what resources are available to students, the steps being taken at the school, an acknowledgement of the loss, and ways in which parents can help their children cope with the incident. Also, provide on the back of the letter a list of community resources.

Offer staff debriefing

Staff debriefing is the same as classroom debriefing and should be conducted within the first two or three days of an incident. The format is semi-structured. A counselor, crisis team member, school psychologist, or an external resource person may conduct the debriefing. It is preferable to have an external resource person because a critical incident affects all school staff. Attendance at the debriefing should be strongly encouraged. All teaching and support staff (including secretarial, custodial) should attend. This session may last from one to two hours.

Hold an operational debriefing

The operational debriefing, like the classroom debriefing, follows a structured format to debrief school-based and district/division crisis response teams. The debriefings should be conducted at their respective locations. School-based and district/division teams should not be debriefed together. The principal or counselor may conduct the debriefing at the school, or an external resource person may be asked to conduct it. Likewise, the district/division crisis team leader or external resource person should conduct the district/division debriefing. The debriefing should occur within two weeks after the incident has passed. These teams are concerned with improving their future performance during a crisis.

CHOOSE THE FORMS YOU WILL USE

A short description and rationale for the most often used forms is provided below. Each form can be modified to meet your needs. Note that descriptions are not provided for the rapid response checklists, except for those that are used during immediate response.

If you wish an electronic copy of these forms, please contact either of the authors by e-mail. Electronic versions allow modifications of the forms to specific settings, and also allow school officials to complete them online, when appropriate. The original purchaser of this book is given permission to copy forms for crisis intervention purposes.

> *Note: The checklists, logs, records, and forms in this book are included as a guide only. It is the responsibility of the principal, in collaboration with the school crisis team, to determine which will be used.*

Rapid response checklists

The rapid response checklists listed below are located in Appendix 2. They can be used when you want to ensure that specific steps and actions have taken place.

Note that descriptions are not provided for all rapid response checklists, only those that are used during immediate response.

Immediate response checklists

- Immediate response checklist
- Immediate response contact information list
- School/community crisis response team contact information list
- Telephone contact tree
- Checklist for handling the media

Crisis-specific checklists

- Violence-specific checklist
- Threat-assessment checklist
- Suicide-specific checklist
- Sudden loss checklist
- Large-scale disaster checklist
- Marine disaster checklist

Assessment-related checklists

- Initial assessment checklist
- Individual assessment checklist
- Suicide risk assessment checklist
- Teacher's checklist
- Threat assessment checklist

Intervention-related checklists

- Age-specific support strategies checklist
- Group debriefing checklist
- Classroom debriefing checklist
- Individual debriefing checklist
- Operational debriefing checklist
- Checklist for handling the media

School/community crisis response team contact information list

Complete this to provide a list of the current school-based team members and their chief responsibilities. Space is provided for alternate members.

Telephone contact tree

This form provides a quick and systematic process for contacting all staff should a critical incident occur after hours.

Crisis information form

This form should be completed and sent off to the area superintendent. It contains all the essential information about the current critical incident.

Initial crisis management plan

Completion of this form provides a detailed record of the known facts about the critical incident, role responsibilities, activities for children, response to media, considerations about a memorial, and more. This form should be retained at the school. It will assist the principal when developing a response plan to a critical incident, and serve as a permanent record in case of any discrepancy. It may serve as the school critical incident plan or be used as additional or preliminary information when developing a plan for the school.

Day 1 operational checklist

This checklist contains most of the important actions and considerations that should take place the first day when responding to a critical incident. It is in checklist format and every item is either checked off yes or no. This makes it quick to complete and easy to scan to determine which actions have or have not been taken. Most school crisis intervention plans tend to be different from each other. Some items on this checklist may not be included in your school crisis plan. Some may not be checked off because it has been determined that the action is not necessary for the current situation. Item selection for your school plan will depend upon the nature of the critical incident, the available resources, and individual approach to responding to crises.

Day 2 operational checklist

This checklist contains most of the important actions and considerations that should continue into the second day of a critical incident. Some items on this checklist may not be included in your school crisis plan and some items may not be included because it has been determined that the action is not necessary for the current situation. Item selection for your school plan will depend upon the nature of the critical incident, the available resources, and individual approach to responding to crises.

Day 3 operational checklist

This checklist contains most of the important actions and considerations that should continue into the third day of a critical incident. The focus of some items is toward restoring routine and structure. Some items on this checklist may not be included in your school crisis plan or some may not be checked off because it has been determined that the action is not necessary for the current situation. Item selection for your school plan will depend upon the nature of the critical incident, the available resources, and individual approach to responding to crises.

Telephone log

Complete this to retain a record of all incoming or outgoing calls about the critical incident. You can determine at a glance if a follow-up is required.

Critical incident alert form

This form is completed and sent to all school staff. It provides known information about the critical incident. This will ensure that all staff members have been informed about the facts of the incident.

Classroom support request log

Complete this log to determine which teachers have requested additional support in their classrooms during a critical incident and the support persons assigned to them.

Student sign-out log

This form is used to record the names of students entering and leaving the school during a critical incident. You can record whether parents have been contacted to pick up a student, or if the student left unescorted.

School visitor's log

This form can be used to monitor and record the names of individuals visiting the school during a critical incident.

Critical incident intervention request

The principal may complete this form when specifically requesting crisis intervention assistance from the district/department of education. It is a good idea to complete this form if there are any questions regarding possible litigation. When this form is completed it provides a detailed record of the request.

External support request record

This provides a record of all additional sources of support that have been contacted by the principal to aid the school crisis team. You can quickly determine which sources have been contacted and whether the support has been provided.

Referral for counseling form

Complete this form to record the names of all students referred for counseling during a critical incident. You can note whether parents have been contacted. Names followed by an (*) indicate that they are "high risk" individuals.

Suicide prevention contract

If you are dealing with an individual who has been identified as "at risk" for attempting suicide you may wish to negotiate a contract with them whereby he or she agrees to abide by the conditions set out in that contract.

Classroom announcement form

The principal should complete this form and give it to every classroom teacher. It contains essential information about the critical incident that teachers should present to students in their classrooms. A brief description of teacher responsibilities is included.

Media information release form

This form is used to provide specific information to the media about a critical incident and the response taken at the school level. District/department crisis members may also complete this form. Specific restrictions are stated to the media and their cooperation is requested. For reasons of confidentiality, remember not to state victims' names unless approved by the parents or guardians.

Memorial service record

Complete this form to record all the necessary information about a school-based memorial service.

Critical incident report

Complete this form to provide a summary of the steps taken when responding to a critical incident. Entries do not have to be in-depth, but should provide documented evidence that an intervention or action took place. Completion of this form could be useful if there are concerns about possible litigation. As well, having the steps documented will help in developing and refining your school crisis intervention plan.

Critical incident log

The school crisis team and/or district/department crisis team should use this form to track and record all critical incidents.

Follow-up checklist

Complete this form to ensure that all specified follow-up activities and responsibilities have been completed.

School/community critical incident plan review

Complete this form on an annual or semiannual basis. Use of this form will maintain a degree of quality assurance for your school crisis intervention plan.

References

- Alberta Education Response Center (1992). Bereavement and loss manual: For administration and teachers. Edmonton, Alberta, Canada.

- American Psychiatric Association. (2013). Diagnostic and statistical manual of mental disorders: DSM-5 (5th ed.) Arlington, VA: American Psychiatric Publishing.

- Blurton, J. (January, 2005). Dealing with children and catastrophic events. www.talhk.com.

- Brock, S. E. (2002). Identifying individuals at risk for psychological trauma. In Brock, S. E., Lazarus Jr, P. J., and Jimerson, S. R. (Eds.). Best practices in school crisis prevention and intervention, 367-383. Bethesda, MD: National Association of School Psychologists.

- Cameron, J.K. (2004). Assessing violence potential: Protocol for dealing with high-risk student behaviors, Fourth Edition.

- Cameron, J.K., Sawyer, D., Urbanoski, R.N. (2004). Strategic interviewing in threat assessment Level II.

- Center for Mental Health in Schools at UCLA. (2008). Responding to a crisis at a school. Los Angeles, CA: Author.

- Clayton, J. Crisis intervention guide. Halifax Regional School Board, Nova Scotia, Canada.

- Coquitlam School District (1996). Coping with sudden death in the school setting.

- Cox, G. R., Robinson, J., Williamson, M., Lockley, A., Cheung, Y. T., and Pirkis, J. (2011). Suicide clusters in young people: evidence for the effectiveness of postintervention strategies. Crisis, 33(4), 208-214.

- Delta School District. (2014). School critical incident response protocol. Retrieved from: http://web.deltasd.bc.ca/files/1957_SchoolCriticalIncidentProtocolRevisedFeb2014.pdf

- Everstine, D. S, and Everstine, L. (1993). People in crisis. New York: Brunner and Mazel Inc.

- Fairchild, T.N. (1986). Crisis intervention strategies for school-based school helpers. Illinois: Charles C. Thomas Publishers.

- Flannery, R. B. (1999). Psychological trauma and posttraumatic stress disorder: A review. International Journal of Emergency Mental Health, 1(2), 135-140.

- Goodwin, R. D., and Gotlib, I. H. (2004). Panic attacks and psychopathology among youth. Acta Psychiatrica Scandinavica, 109(3), 216-221.

- Gould, M. S., Midle, J. B., Insel, B., and Kleinman, M. (2007). Suicide reporting content analysis: Abstract development and reliability. Crisis: The Journal of Crisis Intervention and Suicide Prevention, 28(4), 165-174. doi:10.1027/0227-5910.28.4.165

- Greenstone, J. L., and Leviton, S.C. (1993). Elements of crisis intervention. California: Pacific Grove.

- Jimerson, S. R., Brock, S. E., and Pletcher, S. W. (2005). An integrated model of school crisis preparedness and intervention: A shared foundation to facilitate international crisis intervention. School Psychology International, 26(3), 275-296.

- Johnson, K., (1987). Classroom crisis. California: Hunter House.

- Johnson, K., (1989). Trauma in the lives of children. California: Hunter House.

- Johnson, K., (1993). School crisis management. California: Hunter House.

- Knox, K. S., and Roberts, A. R. (2005). Crisis intervention and crisis team models in schools. Children and Schools, 27(2), 93-100.

- Maslach, C., Schaufeli, W. B., and Leiter, M. P. (2001). Job burnout. Annual review of psychology, 52(1), 397-422.

- Mitchell, J. T. (n.d). Critical incident stress debriefing (CISD). Retrieved from: http://www.info-trauma.org/flash/media-e/mitchellCriticalIncidentStressDebriefing.pdf

- Mitchell, J., and Everly, G.S. (1993). Critical incident stress debriefing: An operations manual for the prevention of traumatic stress among emergency service and disaster workers. Ellicott City: Chevron Publications.

- Nickerson, A. B., Brock, S. E., and Reeves, M. A. (2006). School crisis teams within an incident command system. The California School Psychologist, 11(1), 63-72.

- O'Carroll, P. W., Mercy, J. A., Steward, J. A., and Centers for Disease Control. (1988). CDC recommendations for a community plan for the prevention and containment of suicide clusters. Morbidity and Mortality Weekly Reports, 37(8-6), 1-12.

- Payne, A.A. (2008). "A multilevel analysis of the relationships among communal school organization, student bonding, and delinquency." Journal of Research in Crime and Delinquency.

- Pearlman, L. A., and Mac Ian, P. S. (1995). Vicarious traumatization: An empirical study of the effects of trauma work on trauma therapists. Professional Psychology: Research and Practice, 26(6), 558-565. doi:10.1037/0735-7028.26.6.558

- Perry, B. D. (2002). Stress, trauma and post-traumatic stress disorders in children: An introduction. The Child Trauma Academy. Retrieved from: http://www.forallsyrians.net/uploads/1/6/8/5/16859390/trauma3.pdf

- Petersen, S., and Straub, R. L., (1992). School crisis survival guide. New York: The Center for Applied Research in Education.

- Pross, C. (2006). Burnout, vicarious traumatization and its prevention. Torture, 16(1), 1-9.

- Qualicum School District, British Columbia, Canada, (1997). Sudden death/suicide protocols.

- Quick Response: A step-by-step guide to crisis management. District 105, Yakima, Washington

- Ramsay, R., Tanney, B., Tierney, R., and Lang, W., (1994). Suicide Intervention Handbook. Calgary, Alberta, Canada: Living Works Education Inc.

- Rando, Grieving: How to go on living when someone you love dies. Retrieved from: http://smhp.psych.ucla.edu/pdfdocs/crisis/crisis.pdf

- Richards, K., Campanini, C., and Muse-Burke, J. (2010). Self-care and well-being in mental health professionals: The mediating effects of self-awareness and mindfulness. Journal of Mental Health Counseling, 32(3), 247-264.

- Roberts, A., (1990). Crisis intervention handbook: assessment, treatment and research. California: Wadsworth Publishing Company.

- Sandoval, J. (2013). Crisis counseling, intervention and prevention in the schools. Routledge.

- Stamm, B. H. (2005). The ProQOL manual. Retrieved from: http://compassionfatigue. org/pages/ProQOLManualOct05.pdf.

- Steele, W., and Raider, M. (1991). Working with families in crisis. New York: The Guilford Press.

- Stien, P., and Kendall, J. C. (2014). Psychological trauma and the developing brain: Neurologically based interventions for troubled children. New York, NY: Routledge.

- Swanson, S. A., and Colman, I. (2013). Association between exposure to suicide and suicidality outcomes in youth. Canadian Medical Association Journal, 185(10), 870-877.

- Trepper, T.S., McCollum, E. E., Jong, P.E., Korman, H., Gingerich, W., and Franklin, C. (n.d). Solution-focused therapy treatment manual for working with individuals, Research committee of the solution focused brief therapy association. Solution-Focused Brief Therapy Association. Retrieved from: http://www.sfbta.org/research.pdf

- Trippany, R. L., Kress, V. E. W., and Wilcoxon, S. A. (2004). Preventing vicarious trauma: What counselors should know when working with trauma survivors. Journal of Counseling and development, 82(1), 31-37.

- Villarreal, V., and Peterson, L. A. (2015). Crisis Intervention Team Formation: Application of an Urban School District Model. Communiqué, 43(5), 4-6.

- White, P.F. and Peat, D.W. (2005). Critical incident manual. Care Society, Republic of Maldives.

Appendix 1: Pocket reference cards

DEFUSING EMOTIONS

(1) **Ground rules**

- Maintain confidentiality, what is said here stays here.

- No put-downs, no interruptions.

- Speak only for yourself.

(2) **Format**

- Discuss facts and feelings.

- What did you see?

- What have you heard about the incident?

- What did you feel?

(3) **Identify needs**

- Sort out past and present events.

(4) **Reactions**

- Watch for range of individual reactions.

- Note general amusement, numbness, unaffected.

(5) **When it's over**

- Keep discussion gently focused until it goes its normal routine.

- Expect individuals to refer to incident in the future.

(6) **Assessment**

- Determine who needs further support.

GROUP DEBRIEFING

(1) **Ground rules**

- Maintain confidentiality, what is said here stays here.
- No put downs, no interruptions.
- Speak only for yourself.

(2) **Format**

- Discuss facts and feelings.
- What did you see?
- What have you heard about the incident?
- What did you feel?

(3) **Identify needs**

- Sort out past and present events.

(4) **Reactions**

- Watch for range of individual reactions.
- Note general amusement, numbness, unaffected.

(5) **When it's over**

- Keep discussion gently focused until it goes its normal routine.
- Expect individuals to refer to incident in the future.

(6) **Assessment**

- Determine who needs further support.

CLASSROOM DEBRIEFING

(1) **Introduction**

- Lay out ground rules for participation.
- State introduction and purpose.
- Maintain confidentiality, what is said here stays here.
- No put-downs, no interruptions.
- No blaming others.
- Speak only for yourself.
- Pass if you do not want to speak.
- Everyone is equal here.

(2) **Facts**

- Explore/gain consensus on the sequence of events and role each played in the incident.
- What happened?
- Who was involved?
- When did it happen?
- Where did it happen?
- How did it happened?

(3) **Thoughts**

- What was the first thing you thought about?

(4) **Reactions**

- What was the worst thing about the incident?
- What was your first reaction?
- How are you reacting now?
- What effect has this had on you?

(5) **Symptoms**

- Give each student the opportunity to share.

- What unusual things did you experience at the time?

- What unusual things are you experiencing now?

- Has your life changed in any way at home or at school?

(6) **Teaching**

- Provide information regarding normal reactions to the incident and anticipates later reactions.

- Clear up any misconceptions about the incident and its effects.

- Provide assurance that the following feelings, thoughts, and symptoms are 100% normal: denial, avoidance, sleep difficulties, irritability, fatigue, restlessness, depression/mood swings, difficulty concentrating, nightmares, vomiting/diarrhea, suspiciousness.

- How have you coped with difficulties in the past?

- What are you doing to cope now?

- How will you know that things are getting better for you?

(7) **Closure**

- Remind students of their strengths.

- Reassure them that it will take time to heal.

- Reassure them that you will be there.

- Any other questions?

- Want to add something?

INDIVIDUAL DEBRIEFING

(1) **Find privacy.**

- Find a comfortable, private place for debriefing.
- Avoid placing yourself in a compromising position by always staying visible to others.

(2) **Maintain calm.**

- Present a balanced demeanor to let the student that what he or she is about to say will be accepted.

(3) **Be honest with yourself.**

- Stay in touch with your own feelings and reactions to the student, the issues, and the situation.
- If it becomes too much for you, ask someone else to take over and arrange a transition.

(4) **Read between the lines.**

- Watch the student's behavior.
- Be aware of subtle messages.
- Draw inferences for further exploration.

(5) **Validate feelings.**

- Remember that feelings are neither right nor wrong.
- Validate the student by being present, regardless of what feelings are expressed.

(6) **Listen well.**

- Use gentle probes for clarification and elaboration.
- Maintain good eye contact.
- Use increasingly focused questions when appropriate (especially if you suspect harm).
- Trust your hunches, and check them out.

(7) **Show belief.**

- Listen and facilitate expression.
- Do not judge or investigate.
- Show confidence, trust, and faith that the student is speaking the truth as he or she believes it to be.

(8) **Dispel fault.**

- Reassure the student that the incident was not his or her fault. Be proactive about this.

(9) **Explore fears.**

- Facilitate expression of the student's assumptions, questions, and fears about the incident.

(10) **Provide information.**

- If you know something about the incident, normal reactions to that type of incident, or actions that could be taken, consider sharing that information.
- Do not to "preach."
- Be sure that your own need to "do something" does not cloud your judgment regarding the timeliness of the information.

(11) **Walk through the process.**

- In a given situation, many reactions and processes are predictable. Share what you know to help the student to predict and plan for the near future.

(12) **Explore resources.**

- Explore with the student what resources are available, and what his or her personal support system provides.
- Assist the student in deciding when, how, and to whom to reach out for support.

OPERATIONAL DEBRIEFING

(1) **Introduction**

- State purpose of the debriefing.
- State any ground rules.

(2) **Facts**

- Explore/gain consensus on what happened and the sequence of events.
- Review the role each team member played.

(3) **Assessment**

- Review the team performance.
- Acknowledge things done well.
- Identify areas for improvement.

(4) **Reactions**

- Review individual reactions during the incident.

(5) **Interpretation of response**

- Provide opportunity to make sense of/understand the incident from a professional perspective.

(6) **Plans for improvement**

- Identify lessons learned for future crisis response.

(7) **Closing**

- Plan to implement the lessons learned.

ASSESSING RISK OF SUICIDE

(1) **Identify prior suicidal behavior.**

- Have there been previous attempts?

- Is there a family history of suicide?

(2) **Assess level of risk.**

- Does the person have a specific plan?

- Does the person have access to lethal means?

- Has the person completed preparations?

- Has the person chosen a specific time?

(3) **Assess internal and external resources.**

- Low self-esteem and self-confidence?

- Negative outlook on life?

- Unrealistic goals and dreams?

- Poor physical and/or mental health?

- Few friends?

- Dysfunctional family?

- Poor role models to follow?

- No access to professional help?

- Unsatisfying job or academic career?

(4) **Take all threats seriously.**

- The more points, the higher the risk.

- Investigate threats.

Appendix 2: Checklists and forms

HOW TO USE APPENDIX 2

If a critical incident has occurred:

(1) Refer to and use the **immediate response checklists** below. Note that where associated forms exist, titles are formatted with **bold**.

(2) Refer and use to the most appropriate **crisis, assessment, and intervention checklists**.

(3) Refer to and use the appropriate forms for **documentation, record keeping, and follow-up**.

The following checklists and forms are found in this appendix.

Immediate response checklists

- Immediate response checklist
- Immediate response contact information list
- School/community crisis response team contact information list
- Telephone contact tree
- Checklist for handling the media

Crisis-specific checklists

- Violence-specific checklist
- Threat-assessment checklist
- Suicide-specific checklist
- Sudden loss checklist
- Large-scale disaster checklist
- Marine disaster checklist

Assessment-related checklists

- Initial assessment checklist

- Individual assessment checklist
- Suicide risk assessment checklist
- Teacher checklist
- Threat assessment checklist

Intervention-related checklists

- Age-specific support strategies checklist
- Group debriefing checklist
- Classroom debriefing checklist
- Individual debriefing checklist
- Operational debriefing checklist
- Checklist for handling the media

Forms for documentation, record keeping, and follow-up

- Crisis information form
- Initial crisis management plan
- Day 1 operational checklist
- Day 2 operational checklists
- Day 3 operational checklists
- Telephone log
- Critical incident alert form
- Classroom support request log
- Student sign-out log
- School visitor's log
- Critical incident intervention request
- External support request record
- Referral for counseling
- Suicide prevention contract
- Classroom announcement form
- Media information release form
- Memorial service record
- Critical incident report
- Critical incident log
- Follow up checklist
- School/community critical incident plan review

CHECKLISTS TO BE USED DURING IMMEDIATE RESPONSE

Immediate response checklist

Situation: _____

Completed by: _____ Date: _____

☐	Immediately determined the seriousness of the situation.
☐	Called 911 or other emergency number for help, ambulance, physician, police, or fire, as necessary.
☐	Got help for the victim(s) and ensured the safety of everyone else.
☐	Gathered facts and maintained confidentiality where necessary.
☐	If a crime of violence was committed, secured the scene and called police.
☐	Notified families of the individuals involved in the situation.
☐	Contacted the area superintendent.
☐	Assembled school-based crisis team and determined what to do.
☐	Determined whether extra support was needed from the department.
☐	Kept media out of the school.
☐	Prepared a statement for release.
☐	Kept unauthorized people away from the area.
☐	Displayed relevant contact details on a notice board.

Adapted from Educational Service (1997)

Immediate response contact information list

Customize and fill in for your particular circumstances.

Agency or person	Contact name	Phone number	Date
Police			
Fire			
Ambulance			
Poison control			
Crisis line			

Agency or person	Contact name	Phone number	Date
Hospital			
Physician			
Social Worker			
Superintendent			
School board chair			
School council			
School psychologist			
Counselor			
School bus company			
Parents/guardians			
Clergy			
Probation officer			
Band office			
Tribal leader or chief			
Council			
Search and rescue			
Civil aviation authority			
Coast guard			

School/community crisis response team contact information list

Post a copy of this form in the staff room, send a copy to your area superintendent, and retain a copy in the school file.

School / community: _____

School year: _____

Team member names	Responsibility	Home phone	Office phone

Alternate team member names	Responsibility	Home phone	Office phone

Telephone contact tree

Extend a chart like this far enough to fill in the names and telephone numbers for all school staff or community team members. Each person then has three people to call when he or she receives a call about a crisis. Distribute and post.

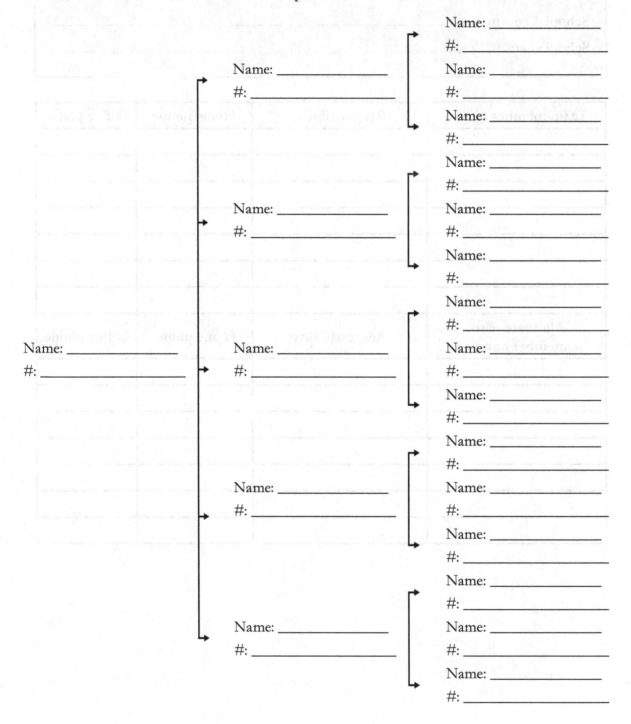

Adapted from Petersen, S., and Straub, R.L. (1992)

Checklist for handling the media

Situation: _____

Completed by: _____ Date: _____

☐	Developed a written statement.
☐	Appointed a spokesperson to speak with media (usually the principal or, if policy dictates, the communications officer).
☐	Kept all staff informed; watched for rumors.
☐	Contacted the press before the press contacted the school.
☐	Set a time and location to meet with the press.
☐	Appointed someone to meet press members and escort them to and from the meeting room.
☐	Set out restrictions for press members while on school property (e.g., not allowed to wander through the school unattended, etc.).
☐	Stressed the positive actions taken by the school in dealing with the incident.
☐	Stressed the services available to students.
☐	Announced changes that took place after the incident had passed.
☐	Clarified any misinformation with the media.

Adapted from Johnson, K. (1993), and Educational Service (1997)

CRISIS-SPECIFIC CHECKLISTS

Violence-specific checklist

Situation: _____

Completed by: _____ Date: _____

☐	Immediately but calmly went to the scene of the violence.
☐	Asked any students remaining in the area to leave.
☐	Did not attempt to take weapon away, if any involved.
☐	Remained calm and called the police.
☐	Did not chase after any individuals who were running away from the scene, but made notes as to whom, what, and where in as much detail as possible.
☐	Conducted an informal assessment of the situation.
☐	Contacted a doctor or called an ambulance if necessary, and made sure that everyone was safe.
☐	If a crime was committed, secured the area and attempted to preserve evidence.
☐	If necessary, called the police or security.
☐	Secured the names of any witnesses and evidence of the crime.
☐	Provided reassurance to the victim(s) that they are safe, and protected them as well as possible.
☐	Did not allow the victim(s) and accused to come into contact.
☐	Expressed to the victim(s) and any witnesses the importance of reporting the incident.
☐	Told the victim(s) to report only the necessary details required.
☐	Maintained the victim's privacy.
☐	Had the victim(s) consult with a lawyer.
☐	If the victim(s) were willing, had them examined by a doctor. (Especially important if a victim was sexually assaulted.)
☐	If domestic violence, helped the person report to the police.

Adapted from Petersen, S., and Straub, R.L. (1992), and Educational Service (1997)

Threat assessment checklist

School/community: _____

Date of threat: _____ Time: _____

Report completed by: _____ Date: _____

Threat maker:

☐   Male   ☐   Female

Birth date (M/D/Y):_____

Age: _____ Grade: _____ Teacher: _____

Home address: _____

_____

Mother: _____

Telephone: (Home) _____ (Office) _____

Father: _____

Telephone: (Home) _____(Office) _____

Family structure:

☐ Single parent	☐ Two parents	☐ Foster parents
☐ Adopted	☐ Grandparents	☐ Siblings

Details:_____

_____

Threat type:

☐   Traditional   ☐   Mixed type   ☐   Non-traditional

Collaterals:

☐   No   ☐   Yes

Details: _____

_____

Target:

☐   Individual (name): _____

☐   Multiple (names): _____

_____

_____

☐ Object (specify):_____

Type of threat:

☐ Direct   ☐ Veiled   ☐ Indirect   ☐ Conditional

Delivery of threat:

☐ Written   ☐ Verbal   ☐ Posted

☐ Drawing   ☐ Internet   ☐ Gesture

Threat details:

_____

_____

_____

_____

_____

_____

_____

Weapon indicated:

☐ No   ☐ Yes

Details: _____

_____

Time frame:

☐ Morning   ☐ Afternoon   ☐ Night

Specific plan:

☐ No   ☐ Yes

Details: _____

_____

Police contacted:

☐ No   ☐ Yes

Specify contact: _____

Police response: _____

_____

_____

Threat assessment team assembled:

☐ Yes   ☐ No

144

Team members:

_____

_____

_____

_____

_____

_____

Risk level:

☐   Immediate: _____

_____

☐   Threat making behaviors (specify): _____

_____

☐   Worrisome behaviors (specify): _____

_____

☐   High-profile worrisome behaviors (specify): _____

_____

Threat maker interviewed:

☐   Yes   ☐   No

Date: _____ Time: _____ Location: _____

How much time do we have? _____

Who interviewed first? _____

Order of interviewing and by whom:

(1) _____

(2) _____

(3) _____

(4) _____

(5) _____

(6) _____

(7) _____

(8) _____

(9) _____

Observations (check all that apply):

- ☐ Low frustration tolerance
- ☐ Poor coping skills
- ☐ Signs of depression
- ☐ Dehumanizing others
- ☐ Sense of entitlement
- ☐ Need for attention
- ☐ Anger problem
- ☐ Inappropriate humor
- ☐ Lack of trust
- ☐ Changed behavior
- ☐ Interest in violence
- ☐ Likes violent entertainment
- ☐ Conduct problems

- ☐ Externalizes blame
- ☐ Failed love relationship
- ☐ Narcissism
- ☐ Lacks empathy
- ☐ Attitude of superiority
- ☐ Low self-esteem
- ☐ Intolerance
- ☐ Manipulates others
- ☐ Closed social group
- ☐ Rigid/opinionated
- ☐ Negative role models
- ☐ Lacks resiliency
- ☐ Suspensions

Pre-existing conditions (check all that apply):

- ☐ Oppositional defiant
- ☐ Mood disorder
- ☐ Child abuse
- ☐ Conduct disorder
- ☐ Depression
- ☐ Suspension

- ☐ Attention deficit hyperactivity disorder
- ☐ Fetal alcohol spectrum disorder
- ☐ Psychopathology
- ☐ Anxiety
- ☐ Probation
- ☐ Other (specify):

Action taken:

_____

_____

_____

_____

_____

Recommendations:

_____

_____

_____

_____

_____

_____

Follow-up:

_____

_____

146

_____

_____

_____

Anniversary date: _____

Suicide-specific checklist

Situation: _____

Completed by: _____ Date: _____

☐	Acknowledged the suicide; did not try to hide or ignore it.
☐	Gathered crisis team together and determined what steps needed to be taken next.
☐	Informed all school staff.
☐	Completed the **Critical incident alert form**.
☐	Identified those students closest to victim and informed them of the suicide in private. These individuals will be most affected by the suicide.
☐	Set up a student drop-in center in the library (secondary school only) to be used by students who are too upset to remain in class.
☐	Kept students in school, unless they were picked up by their parents.
☐	Remained visible and circulated throughout the school, including during class changes and at lunch time.
☐	Kept newspaper and TV reporters out of the school. All media contact restricted to the principal or a designated alternative.
☐	Prepared an information letter and sent to all parents. Letter provides information to help parents support their children during the crisis.
☐	Prepared a letter and to sent it to the victim's parents.
☐	Provided coping strategies to those closest to the deceased to help them deal with the loss and to encourage them to seek help if they need it.

Adapted from Petersen, S., and Straub, R.L., (1992), and Educational Service (1997)

Sudden loss checklist

Situation: _____

Completed by: _____ Date: _____

- ☐ Acknowledged the loss and pain.
- ☐ Told individuals about the signs and symptoms of acute traumatic stress and acute grief response.
- ☐ Told students that counseling is available.
- ☐ Provided the telephone number for the local crisis line.
- ☐ Encouraged parents to help their children cope with the pain by being available and not leaving them alone.
- ☐ Tried to keep the stress down and avoided letting students congregate in large groups, as they tend to become more upset feed off each other's emotions.
- ☐ Provided the telephone number for any support services available.
- ☐ Informed members of the public through the media of positive ways to express their feelings and how to cope with pain.
- ☐ Provided emotional support and counseling where necessary for adults and children.
- ☐ Avoided giving false information.

Adapted from Petersen, S., and Straub, R.L. (1992), and Educational Service (1997)

Large-scale disaster checklist

Situation: _____

Completed by: _____ Date: _____

- ☐ Contacted government officials.
- ☐ Established a hotline for sharing information.
- ☐ Contacted additional doctors.
- ☐ Contacted additional nurses.
- ☐ Identified people with special needs (such as pregnant women, elderly, children, disabled).
- ☐ Are there volunteers/relief workers to work?

☐	Are there people who can provide psychosocial support?
☐	Is there a safe water supply available?
☐	Determined who is responsible for providing accurate information to the public and to affected people.
☐	Is there sufficient food available for the community and relief workers?
☐	Is there sufficient clothing for the community?
☐	Evaluated need for evacuation, and if necessary, arranged transportation.
☐	Are there sufficient hygiene supplies (especially for women) available?
☐	Is there a need for temporary shelters or tents?
☐	Is there sufficient lighting available?
☐	Is there a place to take the injured?
☐	Are there sufficient medical supplies?
☐	Is there a fear of disease outbreak?
☐	Has a vaccination program started and for which diseases?
☐	Have the relief workers been vaccinated?
☐	Is there a place to store the dead and provide proper burial rites?
☐	Are people available to help store or bury the dead?
☐	Evaluated need for transportation, and if necessary, arranged transportation by sea/air/land.
☐	Is an alternative means of communication available (such as mosque loud speakers or school PA system)?
☐	Is there sufficient security at temporary shelter "camps"?
☐	Is there shelter for the relief workers?
☐	Is the media present? (Use the media to make public announcements about public health issues.)
☐	Is someone responsible for releasing information to the media?
☐	Is there a need to create a team of volunteers to organize various tasks?
☐	Are there donors for food and water?
☐	If communications are cut off, have arrangements been made for transportation to a location where information can be exchanged and gathered?
☐	Has the Department of Health been contacted?
☐	Set up a crisis management task force.
☐	Set up a shelter for foreign aid and supplies and managed it.
☐	Make public announcements about the disaster.

Adapted from White and Peat (2005)

Marine disaster checklist

Situation: _____

Completed by: _____ Date: _____

☐	Clarified the seriousness of the situation.
☐	Determined the location, water conditions, number of people involved, and weather.
☐	Called emergency numbers, coast guard, police, or nearby resorts for help.
☐	Identified possible alternatives to the coast guard for immediate support.
☐	Called nearest hospital and health centers and made sure they are prepared.
☐	Made alternative arrangements for patients if hospitals have insufficient room.
☐	Assembled crisis team members.
☐	Informed the families involved with individuals on the vessel, and gave them contact numbers for updates and accurate information.
☐	Gathered facts and kept in contact with all appropriate authorities (transportation ministry, police, and coast guard) for regular updates.
☐	Arranged for or provided psychosocial support for victims.
☐	Contacted counselors, teachers, and other sources of support in the community and prepared them to offer support.
☐	Kept media away from those close to the victims.
☐	Prepared a news release.

Adapted from White and Peat (2005)

ASSESSMENT-RELATED CHECKLISTS

Initial assessment checklist

Situation: _____

Completed by: _____ Date: _____

☐	Will this situation affect the whole school community?
☐	Might this situation get worse very quickly?
☐	Might this situation recur?
☐	Might this situation get out of control?
☐	Is this situation susceptible to rumors and hysteria?
☐	Is the event seen as important and threatening?
☐	Is there evidence of strong emotional reactions?
☐	Have normal coping behaviors been ineffective?
☐	Is emotional discomfort increasing?
☐	Is there evidence of repeated use of ineffective coping behaviors?
☐	Is disorganization/psychological imbalance occurring?
☐	Is turmoil increasing?
☐	Has the school crisis team been activated?
☐	Is assistance needed from the divisional/department crisis team?
☐	Are rival gangs involved?
☐	Is discipline or crowd control going to be a problem?
☐	Did anyone witness the incident?
☐	Located and spoke with individual(s) who witnessed the incident.
☐	Are the witnesses traumatized?
☐	Are there any groups that will be impacted?
☐	Are there any racial, cultural, or ethnic factors that may affect the situation?
☐	Is the school safe for students?
☐	Are staff members safe?
☐	Are extra monitors required in classrooms?

☐	Are some classes likely to be effected more than others?
☐	Are there any staff members or adults who may be affected more than others?
☐	Are there any legal issues that could affect operation of the crisis team?
☐	Are some places/locations likely to be affected more than others?
☐	Is there any fear that weapons are in the school?
☐	Is there a need to call the police?

Adapted from Fairchild, T.N. (1996), and Educational Service (1997)

Individual assessment checklist

Name of assessed individual: _____

Completed by: _____ Date: _____

Indications of moderate impairment during incident

☐	The individual was confused.
☐	The individual had difficulty solving problems.
☐	The individual had difficulty prioritizing tasks.
☐	The individual exhibited time distortions.
☐	The individual exhibited signs of short-term memory loss.
☐	The individual exhibited signs of fear and anxiety.
☐	The individual exhibited signs of anger.
☐	The individual was irritable.
☐	The individual was easily frustrated.
☐	The individual complained of headaches.
☐	The individual complained of heart palpitations.
☐	The individual exhibited signs of muffled hearing.
☐	The individual complained of having nausea and cramps.
☐	The individual exhibited signs of rapid breathing.
☐	The individual was lethargic, wandering about aimlessly.
☐	The individual appeared to feel dejected.

Indications of moderate impairment after incident

- ☐ The individual expressed fear of going crazy.
- ☐ The individual was preoccupied with the incident.
- ☐ The individual's orientation was constantly towards the past.
- ☐ The individual denied the importance of the incident.
- ☐ The individual had difficulty concentrating on tasks.
- ☐ The individual appeared to be depressed.
- ☐ The individual expressed guilt about the incident.
- ☐ The individual was afraid a similar incident would happen again.
- ☐ The individual had phobic reactions.
- ☐ The individual was suspected of having engaged in substance abuse.
- ☐ The individual exhibited signs of self-destructive behavior.
- ☐ The individual was withdrawn.
- ☐ The individual exhibited sudden changes in lifestyle.
- ☐ The individual had difficulty sleeping.
- ☐ The individual experienced flashbacks and nightmares.
- ☐ The individual showed signs of clingy behavior, regressive behavior, bed wetting, thumb-sucking.
- ☐ The individual experienced a loss of interest in daily activities.
- ☐ The individual had trouble making simple decisions.
- ☐ The individual showed a loss of interest in pleasurable activities.
- ☐ The individual experienced a change in appetite.

Indications of serious impairment after incident

- ☐ The individual could not tell name, date, or the event.
- ☐ The individual exhibited signs of exclusive preoccupation with the event.
- ☐ The individual denied that the event occurred.
- ☐ The individual experienced hallucinations.
- ☐ The individual experienced paralysis.
- ☐ The individual was disconnected from surroundings.
- ☐ The individual acted on bizarre beliefs.
- ☐ The individual was hysterical.

	The individual threatened others.
☐	The individual threatened others.
☐	The individual exhibited signs of physical shock.
☐	The individual got into the fetal position.
☐	The individual experienced panic attacks.
☐	The individual exhibited signs of unfocused agitation.
☐	The individual exhibited ritualistic acting out of the event.
☐	The individual had difficulty caring for him-/herself.

Adapted from Johnson, K. (1993), and Educational Service (1997)

Suicide risk assessment checklist

Name of assessed individual: _____

Completed by: _____ **Date:** _____

The symbol ● indicates that the item is a significant factor or indicator. There are 13 significant indicators in the list. Total the significant indicators that are checked off (bottom).

☐	●	Does the person have a specific plan?
☐	●	Does the person have the means to carry out the plan?
☐	●	Is the person prepared to commit suicide?
☐	●	Has the person set a specific time to commit suicide?
☐	●	Has the person tried to commit suicide before?
☐	●	Is there a history of suicide in the person's family?
☐	●	Does the person have low self-esteem?
☐		Does the person have a negative outlook on life?
☐		Does the person have unrealistic goals and dreams?
☐	●	Does the person have poor physical health?
☐	●	Does the person have poor mental health?
☐	●	The person does not have friends and resources to talk with.
☐	●	Does the person come from a dysfunctional family?
☐		The person does not have a permanent home.
☐		The person does not have access to professional help.

☐		The person does not have positive role models to follow.
☐	●	The person has started to make final arrangements.
☐	●	The person has lost a significant friend, etc. recently.
☐		The person is withdrawn, has decreased social activity.
☐		The person exhibits mood swings.
☐		The person is taking unwarranted risks.
☐		The person expresses self-dislike, "I hate myself."
☐		The person has a pattern of alcohol and drug abuse.

Adapted from Ramsay, R., Tanney, B., Tierney, R., and Lang, W., (1994), and Educational Service (1997)

Number of significant indicators (●) checked off: ____/13

Teacher's checklist

Situation: _____

Completed by: _____ Date: _____

☐	Read the information on the **Critical incident alert form** to the class.
☐	Took a moment to share my feelings with the class.
☐	Told the students about any changes in the classroom and school schedule.
☐	If needed, told the class that a notice about the memorial service would be announced as soon as it was available.
☐	If appropriate, told students not to contact the family of the deceased to seek additional information.
☐	Informed students that they would need permission from their parents to be excused from school to attend a funeral service.
☐	Allowed time for any discussions that students wanted to have.
☐	Wrote down questions that I could not answer and told students that I would get back to them later.
☐	Told class members that if they heard any rumors, they should verify the information with me.
☐	Told students that some may expect to have trouble sleeping, eating, or concentrating.
☐	Announced where the student drop-in center is set up.
☐	Asked the students to support each other.

☐	Suspended any testing and reviews.
☐	Maintained a relaxed structure and routine during the day.
☐	Suggested concrete activities for students to work on.
☐	Asked students how they were going to cope at home.

Adapted from Educational Service (1997)

INTERVENTION-RELATED CHECKLISTS

Age-specific support strategies checklist

Preschoolers 3-6 years /after incident

☐	Limited their exposure to news about the incident from TV, books, and papers.
☐	Encouraged them to draw pictures, make cards, or write a letter.
☐	Answered questions calmly and with limited scope.
☐	Spent extra time with children (e.g., cooking, playing games).
☐	Reassured them that they are safe.
☐	Did not minimize the event.
☐	Did not lie or minimize my own feelings.
☐	Did not make fun of regressive behaviors such as sucking thumb.
☐	Validated their feelings.
☐	Called the disaster by its name, not some other name.
☐	Reassured them about the unusual nature of the event.
☐	Reassured them that this recent event is gone.

School-aged 6-12 years /after incident

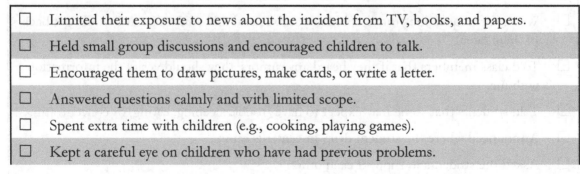

☐	Limited their exposure to news about the incident from TV, books, and papers.
☐	Held small group discussions and encouraged children to talk.
☐	Encouraged them to draw pictures, make cards, or write a letter.
☐	Answered questions calmly and with limited scope.
☐	Spent extra time with children (e.g., cooking, playing games).
☐	Kept a careful eye on children who have had previous problems.

☐	Reassured them that they are safe.
☐	Did not minimize the event.
☐	Did not lie or minimize my own feelings.
☐	Did not make fun of regressive behaviors such as sucking thumb.
☐	Validated their feelings.
☐	Called the disaster by its name, not some other name.
☐	Reassured them about the unusual nature of the event.
☐	Reassured them that this recent event is gone.

Adolescents 12-18 years /after incident

☐	Limited their exposure to news about the incident from TV, books, and papers.
☐	Encouraged them to draw pictures, make cards, or write a letter.
☐	Answered questions calmly and with limited scope.
☐	Spent extra time with children (e.g. cooking, playing games).
☐	Reassured them that they are safe.
☐	Did not minimize the event.
☐	Did not lie or minimize my own feelings.
☐	Did not make fun of regressive behaviors such as sucking thumb.
☐	Validated their feelings.
☐	Called the disaster by its name, not some other name.
☐	Reassured them about the unusual nature of the event.
☐	Reassured them that this recent event is over.
☐	Held small groups to discuss the unusual nature of the crisis.
☐	Discussed the political, psychological, and religious implications of the crisis.
☐	Did not allow scary, dramatic, or inflammatory talk about crisis.
☐	Expected decline in individual work performance.
☐	Kept a special focus on children who were previously emotionally vulnerable or who are currently experiencing emotional difficulty.
☐	Watched for any signs of self-blame or self-criticism.
☐	Watched for any signs of increased irritability, and if evident, explained the cause.

Adapted from Jadis Blurton, Ph.D.

Group debriefing checklist

Situation: _____

Completed by: _____ **Date:** _____

☐ Located private room in which to conduct group discussions.

☐ Kept group sizes to about fifteen to twenty individuals. Included parents if they were at the school.

☐ Kept everyone together for some time.

☐ Stated the ground rules: Maintain confidentiality; no interruptions or put-downs; speak only for yourself.

☐ Kept the discussion focused and avoided tangents.

☐ Encouraged students to talk about the incident by asking direct and explicit questions, such as, "What was the worst part for you?" and "Where were you when it happened?"

☐ Discussed individual reactions to the incident by providing the opportunity for all participants to say: when they heard about the incident, what they heard about the incident, and what they felt.

☐ Prepared students and parents for possible reactions, including: sleeplessness, lack of concentration, nausea, crying, irritability, demanding, fear and anxiety, nightmares, sweating, numbness, withdrawal, and clinginess.

☐ Told them that the above reactions are normal.

☐ Gave suggestions for coping.

☐ Told them that a follow-up would be provided.

☐ Determined which individuals need additional support.

☐ Identified individuals who need ongoing counseling.

☐ Gave counselor names of those individuals needing ongoing counseling.

☐ Contacted parents of individuals having difficulty coping.

Adapted from Johnson, K. (1993), and Educational Service (1997)

Classroom debriefing checklist

Situation: _____

Completed by: _____ Date: _____

☐	Stated the ground rules before starting the debriefing, including: No parents in these sessions; maintain confidentiality; no interruptions or put-downs; speak only for yourself and pass if you do not wish to speak.
☐	Clearly stated the facts of the incident, including what happened; who was involved in the incident; where were you when it occurred; and what role did you play in the incident?
☐	Asked questions to bring out feelings about the incident, such as: How did you first react when you heard the news? What thoughts have you had? What ideas do you think about? How are you reacting now? What effect has this had on you?
☐	Cleared up any misconceptions about the incident.
☐	Explained possible reactions to the incident and normalized reactions by asking questions such as: What symptoms you are experiencing now? How have you coped with difficulties before? What are you doing to cope now? What effect has the incident had on your life.?
☐	Explained the grief cycle and the signs/symptoms of post-traumatic stress syndrome.
☐	Verified that everyone has a trusted person to talk to.
☐	Closed the session with a reminder of individual strengths and that it will take time to heal.
☐	Reassured them that I will be there.

Adapted from Johnson, K. (1993), and Educational Service (1997)

Individual debriefing checklist

Name of debriefed individual: _____

Completed by: _____ Date: _____

☐	Met in a quiet, private location, but within the view of others.
☐	Remained calm when listening to the student.
☐	Kept in touch with my own feelings and reactions to the student and incident.
☐	Watched the student's behavior and looked for hidden messages.

☐	Validated the student's feelings. Feelings are neither right nor wrong.
☐	Listened well, maintained good eye contact, and asked gentle, probing questions.
☐	Showed belief and confidence in what the student told me.
☐	Dispelled fault. Did not let the student take the blame for the incident.
☐	Explored the individual's fears associated with the incident.
☐	Provided information about normal reactions.
☐	Explained the grief process.
☐	Determined whether the individual has access to resources.

Adapted from Johnson, K. (1993), and Educational Service (1997)

Operational debriefing checklist

Situation: _____

Completed by: _____ Date: _____

☐	Clearly stated the purpose of the debriefing.
☐	Stated the ground rules for the debriefing.
☐	Restated the facts of the recent critical incident.
☐	Ensured that team members gained consensus about what happened.
☐	Ensured that team members gained consensus about the order in which things happened.
☐	Restated the role and responsibility of each team member.
☐	Reviewed overall team performance.
☐	Determined which things were done well. Gained consensus from team members.
☐	Determined areas that needed improvement. Gained consensus from team.
☐	Determined individual reactions during the incident.
☐	Ensured that each team member made sense of the incident from a professional perspective.
☐	Ensured that each team member understood the incident and his/her response to it.
☐	Determined what lessons the team had learned from the incident.
☐	Determined what team changes needed to be made for future crisis response.
☐	Developed a plan to implement the changes learned from the recent critical incident.

Adapted from Johnson, K. (1993), and Educational Service (1997)

FORMS FOR DOCUMENTATION, RECORD KEEPING, AND FOLLOW-UP

Crisis information form

(To be completed without prejudice)

Adapted from Petersen, S., and Straub, R.L. (1992)

CONFIDENTIAL

Completed by: _____ Date: _____

Background information:

Victim names	School / community	Grade	Date of birth	Gender

Family constellation:

Mother: _____

Father: _____

Sisters: _____

Brothers: _____

Others: _____

_____

Incident facts (who, what, where, when, how, witnesses, others involved, relationships):

_____

_____

_____

_____

_____

_____

_____

_____

_____

_____

_____

_____

_____

Contacts checklist and details:

✓	Agency or person notified	Contact name	Date / Time	Phone Number
	Police			
	Parent or guardian			
	Superintendent			
	Band office			
	Social worker			
	Nurse			
	Family services			
	Mental health			
	Tribal chief			
	Council			
	Government official			

✓	Agency or person notified	Contact name	Date / Time	Phone Number
	Other			

Notes:

_____

_____

_____

_____

_____

_____

_____

_____

_____

_____

_____

_____

_____

_____

Initial crisis management plan

(To be completed without prejudice)

Adapted from Petersen, S., and Straub, R.L. (1992)

Situation: _____	
Completed by: _____ Date: _____	

Crisis team:

Name	Telephone	Address

Checking the facts of the crisis:

Police contact person: _____

Area superintendent: _____

Other contact persons: _____

_____

_____

Coroner/Medical Examiner: _____

Incident facts (who, what, where, when, how, witnesses, others involved, relationships):

_____

_____

_____

_____

_____

_____

_____

_____

_____

_____

_____

_____

Announcing the event to the school:

How will you tell the staff? _____

_____

Place: _____

Time: _____

Method of contact (include telephone tree): _____

_____

Person presiding: _____

How will you announce the event to students? _____

_____

_____

Method of contact: _____

_____

_____

Person(s) announcing: _____

_____

Place: _____

Time: _____

Written announcement prepared: _____

_____

_____

_____

_____

_____

_____

_____

Teachers' responsibilities:

Check off what you want the teachers to do during the crisis.

☐	Announce event in classroom.
☐	Identify students in need of counseling.
☐	Notify counselor of the number of students wanting counseling.
☐	Remove distraught students from the class and escort to counseling.
☐	Discuss the crisis (refer to suggestions).
☐	Postpone testing.
☐	Eliminate, shorten, and structure assignments for a few days.
☐	Involve class in constructive activities relating to the event (refer to suggestions).
☐	Discuss with students and prepare them for funeral attendance, if needed.
☐	Remove personal items from victim's desk.

Counselor's responsibilities:

Check off what you want the counselors to do during the crisis.

☐	Inform feeder schools so they can provide support for affected students.
☐	Maintain a list of students counseled.
☐	Call parents of students counseled and provide suggestions as to how they can support their children if they are very distressed
☐	If there has been a death, select and inform those students who should participate in the memorial service in either an active or advisory capacity.
☐	Set up and monitor student drop-in center.
☐	Conduct defusing sessions, group discussions, and debriefings.

Reschedule the following activities:

_____

_____

_____

_____

_____

_____

_____

Identify individuals who can work with students

Name: _____ Phone #: _____

Name: _____ Phone #: _____

Name: _____ Phone #: _____

Name: _____ Phone #: _____

Name: _____ Phone #: _____

Principal's responsibilities:

- ☐ Assign extra secretarial help for office or counselor (person and phone).
- ☐ Contact district personnel for support if needed.
- ☐ Stop notifications of student activity (scholarship reports, testing, placement, and attendance) from being sent to the home of a family whose child has died.
- ☐ Arrange for substitute teachers if needed.
- ☐ Contact area superintendent.
- ☐ Prepare information letter to send off to parents.
- ☐ Prepare media statement.

Name: _____ Phone #: _____

Name: _____ Phone #: _____

Name: _____ Phone #: _____

Name: _____ Phone #: _____

Rearrange seating, classes, programs, etc., as indicated by crisis. Changes to be made:

_____

_____

_____

_____

Establish staff and locations for counseling and student drop-in center:

Name: _____ Location: _____

Name: _____ Location: _____

Name: _____ Location: _____

Name: _____ Location: _____

Keep staff updated:

_____

_____

Identify faculty and staff in need of counseling:

_____

_____

_____

_____

Emphasize facts and squelch rumors:

_____

_____

_____

Remain highly visible:

_____

_____

If needed, arrange for excused absences and transportation for students attending off premises funeral.

_____

_____

_____

Arrange for staff debriefing:

Where: _____

When: _____

Person presiding: _____

Contact parents of students who have died:

Name: _____ Phone #: _____

Name: _____ Phone #: _____

Name: _____ Phone #: _____

Name: _____ Phone #: _____

Handling the media:

Spokesperson appointed: _____

Alternate appointed: _____

Person appointed to escort media: _____

People to handle the telephone: _____

_____

_____

_____

Message to be given over the telephone: _____

_____

_____

_____

_____

Media information release developed (complete **Media information release form**):

_____

_____

_____

_____

_____

_____

_____

_____

Establish time and location to meet media: _____

Person appointed to speak to concerned parents: _____

Memorial service:

Is a memorial service indicated in this crisis? _____

Number of students to attend: _____

Location: _____

Person presiding: _____

Speakers: _____

_____

_____

_____

Coordinator: _____

Student involvement:

Name: _____ Role: _____

Name: _____ Role: _____

Name: _____ Role: _____

Name: _____ Role: _____

Name: _____ Role: _____

Name: _____ Role: _____

Activities: _____

_____

_____

_____

_____

_____

_____

Area for staff and students not wishing to participate: _____

_____

_____

Community people who should be invited:

Name: _____ Phone #: _____

Name: _____ Phone #: _____

Name: _____ Phone #: _____

Name: _____ Phone #: _____

Adapting the plan to fit the crisis:

_____

_____

_____

_____

_____

_____

_____

_____

_____

_____

_____

_____

_____

Day 1 operational checklist

Below are 48 items to monitor when developing an operational plan for the first day after a critical incident.

Situation: _____
Completed by: _____ **Date:** _____

☐	Verified information and checked the facts of the incident with police.
☐	Contacted the area superintendent.
☐	Completed the crisis information form and sent it to area superintendent.
☐	Met with all teaching and support staff to announce crisis before school started.
☐	Met with the school crisis intervention team before school started.
☐	Identified high-risk individuals and relatives closest to the victim.
☐	Contacted feeder schools.
☐	Developed a list of staff who may need support in the classroom.
☐	Determined if school-based crisis team can handle critical incident.
☐	Established a central control point for entry to and exit from the school.
☐	Set up a sign in/out log for students picked up/dropped off by parents.
☐	Set up a telephone log to track all inquiries about the incident.
☐	Developed approved information statement to be given out over telephone.
☐	Clearly stated procedure for handling requests and calls from parents and media.
☐	Assigned staff person to retrieve students if parents want to remove them from school.
☐	Requested help with debriefing activities from counselors at feeder schools.
☐	Brought in extra support staff for the front office.
☐	Brought in substitute teachers familiar with the school and students to provide support in classrooms requesting aid.
☐	Set up a student drop-in center (secondary schools only).

☐ Set up a rotation schedule for staff working in student drop-in center.

☐ Set up counseling areas and assigned staff.

☐ Assigned hall and washroom monitors to keep students from wandering.

☐ Assigned roles and responsibilities to all staff.

☐ Commenced defusing emotions sessions.

☐ Assigned debriefing teams and started classroom debriefings.

☐ Developed a list of students absent.

☐ Developed a list of students who attended counseling.

☐ Developed a list of students who require further counseling.

☐ Contacted all parents of any students having difficulty coping.

☐ Developed a list of staff persons absent.

☐ Developed a list of staff persons who may need counseling.

☐ Assigned staff person to remove victim's personal effects from locker.

☐ Prepared a statement for the media regarding the response at the school.

☐ Contacted the media and arranged time and location for meeting.

☐ Assigned a staff person to escort media to and from the front door before and after the meeting.

☐ Scheduled a follow-up meeting time and location with media.

☐ Prepared information letter to parents to be sent home with all students.

☐ Contacted the school bus company about the incident and cautioned about possible changes in students' behavior.

☐ Instructed teachers to postpone testing and have lower expectations for students.

☐ Established a waiting area for parents who come to the school.

☐ Assigned front office staff to escort parents to waiting area.

☐ Ensured that there are light refreshments in the parent waiting area.

☐ Informed school council that the crisis plan had been implemented.

☐ Ensured ongoing contact and support for caregivers.

☐ Scheduled breaks for all staff.

☐ Met with all staff after school to update.

☐ Met with school crisis team after school to re-evaluate plan.

☐ Scheduled staff debriefing date for all teaching and support staff.

☐ Other:

☐ Other:

☐	Other:
☐	Other:
☐	Other:
☐	Other:
☐	Other:

Day 2 operational checklist

Below are 23 items to monitor when developing an operational plan for the second day after a critical incident.

Situation: _____

Completed by: _____ Date: _____

☐	Met with all staff and updated before school started.
☐	Met with the school crisis team before school started and re-evaluated response plan.
☐	Maintained student drop-in center.
☐	Continued to provide classroom support for teachers requesting it.
☐	Continued to have staff person monitor hallways and washrooms.
☐	Maintained telephone log.
☐	Maintained sign in/out log for students leaving the school.
☐	Continued defusing sessions.
☐	Continued classroom debriefing sessions.
☐	Continued student counseling sessions.
☐	Maintained central entry to and exit from the school.
☐	Continued to maintain a list of students who attended counseling.
☐	Continued to keep extra front office staff.
☐	Maintained the parent reception area.
☐	Continued to have a front office staff person escort parents to reception area.
☐	Continued to provide light refreshments in parent area.
☐	Continued to provide light refreshments for staff and support workers.
☐	Contacted parents of the victim and determined their wishes about disposition of personal effects and response by school and students.

☐ In the event of a death, determined which students wanted to attend the funeral.

☐ In the event of a death, ensured that students attending the funeral had been prepared for what to expect.

☐ Met with all staff after school to update.

☐ Met with school crisis team after school to re-evaluate plan.

☐ Scheduled staff debriefing for after school.

☐ Other:

☐ Other:

☐ Other:

☐ Other:

Day 3 operational checklist

Below are 12 items to monitor when developing an operational plan for the third day after a critical incident.

Situation: _____

Completed by: _____ Date: _____

☐ Met with and updated all school staff before school started.

☐ Met with school crisis team before school started and re-evaluated response plan.

☐ Assigned staff person to clear out victim's desk.

☐ Saved victim's personal belongings for parents.

☐ In the event of a death, discussed with staff plans for a school memorial service.

☐ Identified students who wanted to attend the memorial service.

☐ Met with counselor(s) and determined which students need further assistance.

☐ Instructed teaching staff to resume more structure and routine in class.

☐ Scheduled a follow-up meeting with school staff to occur two weeks after the incident.

☐ Re-evaluated response to determine if there are any points not dealt with adequately.

☐ Maintained student drop-in center.

☐ Compiled a list of students wishing to attend the funeral (parental permission required).

☐ Other:

☐	Other:	
☐	Other:	
☐	Other:	
☐	Other:	
☐	Other:	
☐	Other:	
☐	Other:	

Telephone log

School: _____ Sheet #: _____

Start date: _____ End date: _____

Date Time	Name Phone number	Inquiry	Followed up
			☐
			☐
			☐
			☐
			☐
			☐
			☐
			☐
			☐

Date Time	Name Phone number	Inquiry	Followed up
			☐
			☐
			☐
			☐
			☐
			☐
			☐
			☐
			☐
			☐
			☐

Critical incident alert form

Date: _____ Time: _____

To: _____

From: _____

School/community: _____

Subject: _____

Verified information:

When: _____

_____

_____

Who: _____

_____

_____

_____

_____

_____

Where: _____

_____

_____

_____

_____

How: _____

_____

_____

_____

_____

_____

_____

_____

Classroom support request log

School: _____ Sheet #: _____

Start date: _____ End date: _____

Room #	Teacher	Person assigned	Duration

Student sign-out log

School: _____ Sheet #: _____

Start date: _____ End date: _____

Date / Time	Name	Parent contacted	Picked up
		☐	☐
		☐	☐
		☐	☐
		☐	☐

Date Time	Name	Parent contacted	Picked up
		☐	☐
		☐	☐
		☐	☐
		☐	☐
		☐	☐
		☐	☐
		☐	☐
		☐	☐
		☐	☐
		☐	☐
		☐	☐
		☐	☐
		☐	☐
		☐	☐
		☐	☐
		☐	☐

School visitors log

School: _____ Sheet #: _____

Start date: _____ End date: _____

Date Time	Initial	Name	Purpose

Date Time	Initial	Name	Purpose

Critical incident intervention request

Request date/time: _____ **Report #:** _____

Requested by: _____ Position: _____

School: _____

Location: _____

Office phone: _____ Home phone: _____

Requested by: _____ Position: _____

School: _____

Location: _____

Office phone: _____ Home phone: _____

Date of incident: _____ Time: _____

Summary of incident: _____

_____

_____

_____

_____

_____

_____

_____

_____

Urgency of request:

☐   Immediate response

☐   Response within seven hours

☐   Response within 24 hours

☐   Response within 48 hours

☐   Response within five days

☐   Follow-up within two weeks

Total number of participants:

Staff: _____ Students: _____ Grade levels: _____

Intervention(s) requested:

☐   Defusing sessions   ☐   Individual counseling

☐   Classroom debriefings   ☐   Operational debriefing

☐   Individual debriefings   ☐   General support

☐   Group discussions   ☐   First Nations consultant

☐   Follow-up   ☐   Other (specify): _____

School crisis team:

Active: ☐   Yes   ☐   No

School crisis team member(s):

(1) _____

(2) _____

(3) _____

(4) _____

(5) _____

School team leader: _____

Contact number: _____

Additional information/instructions:

_____

_____

_____

_____

_____

Signature: _____ Date: _____

External support request record

The resources listed below may be contacted to provide additional support to the school-based crisis response team during a critical incident. Check off each resource that has been contacted and also check off once each resource has responded.

Request date/time: _____ Report #: _____

School/community: _____ Date: _____

Requested by: _____ Position: _____

Support requested		Name	Phone	Responded
☐	Superintendent or designate			☐
☐	School psychologist			☐
☐	Family and children's services			☐
☐	Social service agencies			☐
☐	Youth probation			☐
☐	Mental health services			☐
☐	Substitute teachers			☐

Support requested	Name	Phone	Responded
☐ Secretarial assistance			☐
☐ Custodial assistance			☐
☐ Medical assistance			☐
☐ Nursing assistance			☐
☐ School counselors			☐
☐ Emergency specialists			☐
☐ Police			☐
☐ School council			☐
☐ Parental support			☐
☐ Financial assistance			☐
☐ Maintenance			☐
☐ Other (specify):			☐
☐ Other (specify):			☐
☐ Other (specify):			☐
☐ Other (specify):			☐
☐ Other (specify):			☐

Referral for counseling

School: _____ Sheet #: _____

Start date: _____ End date: _____

Risk level: 1-/Low; 2/Moderate; 3/High

Date Time	Name	Risk level	Parent contacted
			☐
			☐
			☐
			☐
			☐
			☐
			☐
			☐
			☐
			☐
			☐

| Date | Name | Risk | Parent |
Time		level	contacted
			☐
			☐
			☐
			☐
			☐
			☐
			☐
			☐

Suicide prevention contract

I, _____, agree that I will not attempt to commit suicide or hurt myself in any way for the next _____days.

If I feel that I will try to break this contract and I am at school, I will immediately contact _____ at _____.

If I feel that I will try to break this contract and I am not at school, I will immediately contact _____ at _____.

I agree that I will not make any final decision or attempt at committing suicide until I have talked with my counselor/helper directly.

This contract is effective immediately.

Student: _____ Date: _____

Counselor: _____ Date: _____

Classroom announcement form

Please read this information to your class. If you do not feel comfortable presenting this, request assistance.

Note: Simplify the information when debriefing lower elementary grades.

When: _____

Who: _____

Where: _____

_____

How: _____

_____

Student resources: _____

_____

Student drop-in center: _____

☐	Read notice to class.
☐	Conduct classroom debriefing session, defusing, and group discussions.
☐	Allow students to attend student drop-in center (secondary school).
☐	Request classroom support if needed.
☐	Request that a crisis team member read the notice if you are unable to do so.
☐	Suspend any student testing.
☐	Reduce student workload.
☐	Refer students for counseling if needed.
☐	Continue to maintain minimum structure and routine.
☐	Do not allow students to roam the halls.
☐	Identify students at risk.
☐	Take time for yourself.

Media information release form

DO NOT state victim(s) name (unless parent permission given).

Clarify misinformation.

School/community: _____ **Date:** _____	
Location: _____ **Time:** _____	

School spokesperson: _____

Media representatives: _____

Media restrictions:

☐ Access limited to meeting room only.

☐ Wandering about the school is prohibited.

☐ Student interviews are prohibited while on school property.

☐ Staff interviews are prohibited unless approved by the principal.

☐ Photography while on school property is prohibited.

☐ Other:

When: _____

Who: _____

Where: _____

_____

How: _____

_____

Positive action taken: _____

_____

Changes made after incident: _____

_____

Services available to students: _____

_____

Follow-up meeting scheduled: ☐ Yes   ☐ No

Location: _____ Date: _____ Time: _____

Memorial service record

School/community: _____ Location: _____

Service date: _____ Time: _____ Location: _____

Service organizer: _____ Contact number: _____

Total attending: Students _____   Staff _____

Parents attending: ☐   Yes   ☐   No

Transportation required: ☐   Yes   ☐   No

Seating arranged: ☐   Yes   ☐   No

Officiating clergy: _____ Contact number: _____

Officiating clergy: _____ Contact number: _____

Guest speakers:

Name: _____

Name: _____

Student speakers:

Name: _____

Name: _____

Music selections/hymns:

_____

_____

_____

_____

Readings:

_____

_____

_____

_____

Floral arrangements: ☐   Yes   ☐   No

Reception area prepared: ☐   Yes   ☐   No

Refreshments available: ☐   Yes   ☐   No

Student tributes: ☐   Yes   ☐   No

Community guests invited: ☐   Yes   ☐   No

Name: _____

Name: _____

Name: _____

Name: _____

Specific religious concerns/instructions: _____

_____

_____

_____

_____

Waiting area for staff/students not participating: ☐ Yes ☐ No

Location: _____

Critical incident report

Report date: _____ **Report #:** _____

Response start date: _____ **Response start time:** _____

Response close date: _____ **Response close time:** _____

Total response time: (Days) _____ (Hours) _____

School/community initiated request: ☐ Yes ☐ No

District/department initiative: ☐ Yes ☐ No

School/community: _____

Location: _____

Principal/official: _____ Contact number: _____

District/department team dispatched by: _____

Position: _____ Contact number: _____

Summary of incident:

Date: _____ Time: _____

Who: _____

Where: _____

What: _____

How: _____

Victim(s), siblings, witnesses:

- **Ethnicity:** C-Caucasian / NA-Native American / B-Black / A-Asian / I-Indian / O-other

- **Status:** I-Injured / D-deceased
- **Cause:** S-suicide / A-accident / H-homicide / N-natural / I-illness / SL-sudden loss

Victim name	Age	Grade	Ethnicity	Status	Cause
(1) _____	___	___	___	___	___
(2) _____	___	___	___	___	___
(3) _____	___	___	___	___	___
(4) _____	___	___	___	___	___

Sibling(s)/witnesses: ☐ Yes   ☐ No

Name	Age	Grade
(1) _____	___	___
(2) _____	___	___
(3) _____	___	___
(4) _____	___	___

Total injured: _____ Total deceased: _____

Total student population: _____ Total staff: _____

Total number of grades: _____

Crisis teams and external agencies:

School crisis team participation: ☐ Yes   ☐ No

District/department crisis team participation: ☐ Yes   ☐ No

External agency or agencies involved: ☐ Yes   ☐ No

Contact:	Number:
(1) _____	_____
(2) _____	_____
(3) _____	_____
(4) _____	_____

Intervention(s) requested:

☐ Defusing sessions   ☐ Individual counseling

☐ Classroom debriefings   ☐ Operational debriefing

☐ Individual debriefings   ☐ General support

☐ Group discussions   ☐ Follow-up

☐ Other (specify): _____

Team members:

District/department team members:

(1) (Leader)_____

(2) _____

(3) _____

(4) _____

(5) _____

(6) _____

School crisis team members:

(1) (Leader)_____

(2) _____

(3) _____

(4) _____

(5) _____

(6) _____

School memorial service held: ☐ Yes ☐ No

Memorial service date/time: _____

At risk students identified: ☐ Yes ☐ No

Parent(s)/guardian contacted: ☐ Yes ☐ No

Follow-up date(s):

(1) _____

(2) _____

Recommendations: _____

_____

_____

_____

_____

_____

_____

Signature: _____ Date: _____

Witness: _____ Date: _____

192

Critical incident log

| Sheet #: _____ |
| Start date: _____ End date: _____ |

Use the following abbreviations when filling out the form below:

Cause:

- S-suicide / A-accident / H-homicide / N-natural / I-illness / SL-sudden loss

Ethnicity:

- C-Caucasian / NA-Native American / B-Black / A-Asian / I-Indian / O-other

Time:

- Time spent at the school expressed in hours (H) and/or days (D).

Action:

- 1-defusing / 2-group discussion / 3-individual debriefing / 4-classroom debriefing / 5-counseling / 6-general support / 7-Native American consultant / 8-operational debriefing / 9-follow-up / 10-other

Date	General description of incident	Student (STU) or staff (STA)	Injury (I) or death (D)	Cause	Age	Grade	Ethnicity	Time in hours (__H) or days (__D)	Action

Date	General description of incident	Student (STU) or staff (STA)	Injury (I) or death (D)	Cause	Age	Grade	Ethnicity	Time in hours (__H) or days (__D)	Action

Follow-up checklist

Completed by: _____ Date: _____

☐ Recorded the anniversary date of the incident for future reference.

☐ Determined if the counselor saw all students identified as "at risk."

☐ Ensured that parents of all "at risk" students were contacted.

☐ Ensured that all school staff attended a debriefing session within the first week.

☐ Ensured that the school-based crisis team members attended an operational debriefing session within two weeks after the incident.

☐ Scheduled a follow-up session with staff to occur six weeks after the incident.

☐ Sent out personal thank-you notes to all substitutes, teachers, counselors, parents, and organizations that helped in some way during the critical incident.

☐ Other (specify):

☐ Other (specify):

☐ Other (specify):

☐ Other (specify):

☐ Other (specify):

School/community critical incident plan review

Indicate which part(s) and/or procedure(s) of your school critical incident plan have been reviewed, revised, amended, or deleted.

School/community: _____ Date: _____

Action taken by: _____ Position: _____

Start date: _____ Close date: _____

Initial response:

☐	Reviewed (specify):
☐	Revised (specify):
☐	Amended (specify):
☐	Deleted (specify):

Day 1 plan:

☐	Reviewed (specify):
☐	Revised (specify):
☐	Amended (specify):
☐	Deleted (specify):

Day 2 plan:

☐	Reviewed (specify):
☐	Revised (specify):
☐	Amended (specify):
☐	Deleted (specify):

Day 3 plan:

☐	Reviewed (specify):
☐	Revised (specify):
☐	Amended (specify):
☐	Deleted (specify):

Forms:

- [ ] Forms reviewed (specify):
- [ ] Forms revised (specify):
- [ ] Amended (specify):
- [ ] Deleted (specify):

Follow-up:

- [ ] Reviewed (specify):
- [ ] Revised (specify):
- [ ] Amended (specify):
- [ ] Deleted (specify):

Staff training:

- [ ] Reviewed (specify):
- [ ] Revised (specify):
- [ ] Amended (specify):
- [ ] Deleted (specify):

The authors

Peter White and David Peat first met in the 1990s while they were colleague psychologists in the Yukon Territory, Canada. They periodically kept in touch, and finally worked together again in Singapore and the Maldives during 2005. Since then, they continue to collaborate in various ways, despite living in different parts of the world.

PETER WHITE

Peter White is from Nova Scotia, Canada, but moved from Halifax to Whitehorse, Yukon Territory, Canada, in 1991. He was employed by the Yukon Territory's Department of Education Special Programs Branch as an educational psychologist from 1991 until 2014.

Peter completed his Bachelor of Arts degree in Logic and Semantics at Dalhousie University in Halifax, his Bachelor of Education degree at Acadia University in Wolfville, and his Master of Arts degree in Educational Psychology and Measurement at Mount Saint Vincent University in Halifax. Prior to relocating to Whitehorse, Peter worked as an educational psychologist with the Nova Scotia Hospital's psychology department in Dartmouth; as a training officer with the Nova Scotia Hospital's staff development department; and as an educational psychologist with the Terra Nova and Cape Freels Integrated School Boards in Newfoundland. He has also worked as an educational psychologist with the Sooke District School Board on Vancouver Island; the Prince George District School Board in central British Columbia; and as a "freelance" psychologist in Atlin, northern British Columbia, Canada. Internationally, Peter worked as an educational psychologist in Singapore with David Peat, conducting assessments and presenting teacher workshops at international schools. He also assisted in the delivery of post-tsunami train-the-trainer workshops for community-level workers in Male, Republic of Maldives.

Test construction, research design, measurement, and program evaluation are keen interests of Peter's. While working with the Nova Scotia Hospital, he designed and developed the White-Woods Performance Checklist and accompanying training video. This instrument was designed to evaluate one- and two-person cardiopulmonary resuscitation procedures. In addition, he developed (in consultation with the hospital programmer) a computer-based patient tracking system used by one hospital unit, and several checklists for survey research at the Nova Scotia Hospital. As a consultant for the federal government of Canada, Peter designed many performance appraisal instruments (BOS and BARS) to evaluate field-training competence at the individual and group level, and also conducted peer reviews.

Peter has lived and traveled throughout China, lived and worked in Singapore and the Maldives, traveled to the Philippines, Malaysia, Tibet, England, France, Netherlands, Germany, Belgium, Luxembourg, Hawaii, Italy, Austria, Switzerland, Thailand, Cambodia, Laos, and plans to visit many more countries. He is an avid photographer and prefers shooting landscapes, long exposures, and low light as well as architectural images. Photography allows him to combine his love of nature with his passion for photography.

DAVID PEAT

Dr. David Peat has been involved in the fields of education, rehabilitation, and health in various capacities since 1972. Responsibilities within school settings have included being a "mainstream" science, mathematics, and physical education teacher, a "special education" teacher, psychologist, school administrator, district level coordinator of "special services," associate superintendent of schools, and, executive director of research and innovation. Internationally, he has worked extensively in the Middle East and Asia in school, university, government, and mental health settings. Currently, he is an adjunct professor of education at Ambrose University, Calgary, Canada.

After leaving public school teaching in 1984, he returned to university and obtained Masters of Education and Ph.D. degrees. During this time, he also earned an Intercultural Certificate, the qualifications as a reading clinician, and became a chartered psychologist (College of Alberta Psychologists, Canada). As a psychologist, Dr. Peat has worked in various settings throughout Canada, including the remote northern Arctic territory of Yukon. Internationally, he has worked in Kuwait, Qatar, and Singapore in hospital, private school, and government settings. His work emphasized the thorough assessment of abilities to develop appropriate educational, medical, and community-based plans and interventions. Within education ministries in Canada, Dr. Peat has served as a coordinator of special education services and curriculum evaluator. He also is a consultant, helping schools to develop programs and interventions for students with behavioral difficulties; designing and implementing locally developed "thinking-skills" programs; and evaluating special education services.

Working with both experienced and prospective teachers has been a major thrust for Dr. Peat. At the university and college level, he has taught courses entitled Problems of Attention and Behavior; Nature and Characteristics of Learning Disabilities; Educational Procedures for the Learning Disabled; Overview of "Exceptionalities;" and The Diverse Classroom: Curriculum Adaptations and Modifications. Presentations and seminars to schools, teachers, and community agencies in Canada, Kuwait, Qatar, and Singapore have been on topics such as The Direct Instruction of Thinking Skills to Students; Student Assessment; Curriculum Evaluation; Child Development; Parenting; Discipline; Strategic Planning; Stress; Grief and Loss; Post-traumatic stress disorder; Critical Incident Stress Defusing; and How to Design Presentations Based on Adult Learning Principles, to name a few.

From 1997 to 2000, Dr. Peat worked internationally as a psychologist in the Arabian Gulf with the Kuwait-Dalhousie Physiotherapy and Rehabilitation Project, and The Learning Center in Qatar and in Singapore. In Kuwait, his responsibilities included consulting with clinical specialty rehabilitation teams in a hospital setting spanning the areas of neurology, orthopedics, pediatrics, burns, and cardiovascular rehabilitation. Direct patient treatment and family consultations addressed issues such as stress, anxiety, depression, anger management, moving towards the acceptance of disabling conditions, coping with grief and loss, and behavioral issues. Facilitating the development of smooth patient transitions from hospital-based to school and community-based services was a strong focus of his work. Collaborating with health educator Carolyn Madden and clinical teams, they developed and implemented clinical, educational, and preventative programs aimed at helping Kuwaiti citizens lower their risk of disease and/or injury and to adopt healthier lifestyles (e.g., smoking cessation; stress management).

In the educational setting of The Learning Center in Qatar, Dr. Peat, as deputy head and psychologist, was responsible for the oversight, development, and implementation of individual educational plans (IEPs) for children with special needs. He also provided advice to administrators and committees concerning service delivery models and systemic approaches to solving school issues (e.g., bullying). On an individual client basis, he provided psycho-educational assessments for children suspected of having learning disabilities or developmental disabilities; provided counseling services to children and their families; consulted with parents, "regular education" school staff, and other professionals; and conducted in-service education workshops for parents and teachers.

Dr. Peat resided in Singapore from 2000-2006, for the first three years employed as a Senior Educational Psychologist with the Ministry of Education. For the first year, his responsibilities encompassed the development and/or adaptation of Singapore-based and normed assessment instruments in areas such as talent and ability identification, mathematical abilities, and cognitive development. He was also a consultant to gifted education program specialists. The following two years he provided psychological services to schools. He delivered professional development sessions to teachers, parents, and administrators concerning theory and instructional methods for those with learning difficulties (e.g., dyslexia, autism, intellectual disabilities, etc.) and provided advice to policy makers.

From February 2004 to January 2006, he was employed by the Child Guidance Clinic, Institute of Mental Health, Singapore, as the Head and Senior Educational Psychologist responsible for establishing and guiding the COPES (Children's One-stop Psycho-educational Services) program. As well, he was the Academic Director (Education) for James Cook University, Singapore, and taught "Psychological Assessment" to graduate students in the clinical psychology program. When not involved in the above positions, he worked as a "freelance" psychologist, consultant, lecturer, and curriculum and technology developer, translating psychological, instructional, and developmental theory to intervention and practice.

Periodically in 2005-6, through ActionAid International, he trained Maldivian front-line workers, offered post-tsunami psychosocial support to children, and evaluated post-tsunami interventions in India, Sri Lanka, and the Maldives.

As Associate Superintendent of Learning, Rocky View Schools (2006-2010), Dr. Peat was responsible for school division leadership in the areas of curriculum, instruction, and technology to support learning and collaborative partnerships. He guided the implementation of two major initiatives during his tenure:

a) the shift from a "diagnostically-driven" system of support services for students with special needs to a "level of service" model of inclusion where all students receive the required educational, physical, behavioral, and/or social/emotional support required regardless of "diagnostic label," and,

b) the shift to a "future-orientated" school system, supporting the implementation of professional learning systems, teaching methodologies, and technological infra-structure that supports the development of students' skills and abilities aligned with what is required for the 21st century.

Since leaving Rocky View Schools in Canada, as well as being an adjunct Professor of Education at Ambrose University College in Calgary, he is the President of Reach World Wide, an organization dedicated to supporting the transformation of education. In addition, for several months a year, he works in Afghanistan as a Technical Advisor, Curriculum and Instruction, both for the German Government (GIZ) and with T-CAP (Teacher Certification and Accreditation Project – Afghanistan), a project administered by World University Service of Canada (WUSC) and funded by GAF (Global Affairs Canada).

In terms of publications, he is a co-author of a "thinking skills" program entitled SPELT (Strategy Program for Effective Learning and Thinking), which has been implemented with students and teachers in Canada, Korea, India, Australia, New Zealand, and other parts of the world. Ongoing research, coupled with publications in books and journals, spans the topics of literacy, the teaching of thinking skills, curriculum development, instructional practices, change theory, staff development, health and wellness, post-disaster crisis intervention, assessment models/instruments, and most recently, leading entire school systems towards 21st century teaching and learning. His latest co-authored publication is, Ten Strategies for Building Community with Technology: A Handbook for Instructional Designers and Program Developers (Brush Education, 2014).